ROBERT FALLS

AT GOODMAN THEATRE

THE FIRST TWENTY YEARS

"WE STRIVE TO DEFINITIVE EVERY PLAY TO CREATE

CREATE THE PRODUCTION OF

IT FOR ALL TIME—

ENORMOUS IMPRESSION—

A CLASSIC."

"WE COMMIT TO

THROUGHOUT THEIR

TO CREATE A

PASSIONATE

OUR DIRECTORS

CAREERS

BODY OF THEIR MOST

WORK."

"OUR WORK IS A BETWEEN

—INTENSE ENERGY BROUGHT

DIALOGUE
PAST AND PRESENT

TO THE CLASSICS."

"THEATER EXISTS

MOMENTS

THIS IS SIMULTANEOUSLY JOYOUS

PURELY
IN THE MOMENT.
EVAPORATE.
AND SAD."

THE STAGE
PRODUCTION HAS
LASTING DEPTH

NURTURED FOR SO LONG."

"I STRIVE FOR THAT
THEATRICAL

PLAYS THAT CHALLENGE

AND HOW WE

LARGER CONSCIOUSNESS—

OUR IDEAS ABOUT WHO WE ARE
GOT HERE."

ROBERT FALLS
AT GOODMAN THEATRE
THE FIRST TWENTY YEARS

TEXT BY TOM CREAMER, LISA DILLMAN AND STEVE SCOTT

ACKNOWLEDGEMENTS

Designed by The Grillo Group, Inc., Chicago

Separations by Professional Graphics, Rockford, Illinois

Printed and bound in Singapore by CS Graphics Pte. Ltd.

The designers wish to acknowledge the outstanding contributions of Steven E. Gross and Matthew Modine, both of whom have provided photographs for this book. See page 159 for additional photography credits.

Back cover photograph and pages 2–3, 6–11, 14, 22–23, 34–35, 136–137, 146–147 and 160 by Steven E. Gross.

Front cover photograph and pages 4–5 by Matthew Modine.

The following Goodman Theatre staff members have provided many hours of editorial assistance; without their efforts, this book would not have been possible:

Valerie Black-Mallon

Nicole Gilman

Lori Kleinerman

Dorlisa Martin

Julie Massey

Erin Moore

Kelly Rickert

And finally, to the thousands of artists, staff, trustees and contributors who have created the past two decades of work at the Goodman Theatre: our profound thanks.

TABLE OF CONTENTS

Edith-Marie Appleton

The new Goodman Theatre was inspired by the irrepressible dreams, passions and efforts of so many: Artistic Director Robert Falls and the artistic collective; Executive Director Roche Schulfer and the Board of Trustees; and the City of Chicago. But no one provided greater personal support for the state-of-the-art Goodman home on North Dearborn than Edith-Marie Appleton and her son, Honorary Chairman Albert Ivar Goodman.

"We are greatly indebted to Edith-Marie Appleton and Albert Ivar Goodman, who have given our artists a new canvas on which to create the next twenty years of spectacular works that will engage and entertain audiences for decades to come," said Robert Falls.

"Edie was an exceptional and visionary woman who loved people and the performing arts," said Albert Goodman. A native of Evanston, Illinois, she graduated from Smith College in 1941 and then earned a Nursing degree from Evanston Hospital. But she made her career working at Appleton Electric Company, the firm started in 1903 by her father Albert Ivar Appleton.

As Albert grew up, Edie dedicated her time to fundraising—performing in the elementary school fundraising benefit and singing in the Holy Comforter Church choir. However, for a small group of young men, her most memorable role was as den mother for the Wilmette Cub Scouts.

Edie's other interests included fundraising for the Chicago Chapter of the World Adoption International Fund. Later she became involved with such institutions as the Swedish American Museum and Planned Parenthood. In fact, to recognize her Swedish heritage, Albert Goodman and his friends named a stairway in her honor at the Swedish American Museum. A true American, Edie's love of this country is evident in pictures of her that are on display for the troops at the USO of Illinois Center at Navy Pier.

Edie loved the arts. Albert recalls the times that she would play the piano and sing with dinner guests at home. She took Albert to New York to see many Broadway productions.

The key to the "Goodman Connection" was not revealed to Albert until he was nearly grown. While a student at the University of Southern California, he met his paternal grandmother, Ivy Goodman, who told Albert that her husband Robert was a cousin of Kenneth Sawyer Goodman, in whose honor the Goodman Theatre had been founded. This unlocked a new world of cultural experiences for Edie and Albert, and led to their involvement in the new Goodman Theatre. Eventually, they met Robert Falls and Roche Schulfer—and the rest is history.

Albert claims his mother gave him the "greatest gift in the world" by naming the main stage for him. In honor of Edie, Albert gave funds for the Goodman lobby so that her "special smile" would always greet those arriving. In his words, "Edie would be glad that you came back to the Goodman one more time."

Edie represents love, understanding and the importance of a good sense of humor to see you through life's harder times. For the Goodman Theatre, she represents the past, the present and the excitement of a future that's sure to be extraordinary.

Experimental to Acclaimed

In the more than eighty years since its founding, Goodman Theatre has grown from an experimental "art" theater and training center to one of the country's most acclaimed professional theater companies. We are extremely proud to have been a part of the Goodman's evolution, and to have taken part in the extraordinary development of the entire Chicago theater community in the past three decades. In this book, we celebrate the Goodman's heritage with a particular focus on the past twenty years and the artists whose work and talents have created our local, national and international reputation.

It is impossible in a narrative of this length to acknowledge the thousands of artists, trustees, patrons, foundations, corporations, government representatives, volunteers and theater professionals whose dedication and generosity have led to the Goodman's achievements. These are some of our extraordinary leaders:

• Founding Chairman and Life Trustee Stanley M. Freehling.

• Past Chairs and Life Trustees James E. Annable, Sondra A. Healy and Deborah A. Bricker.

• Past Chairs Allen Turner, David Ofner, Irving J. Markin and Carol Prins.

• Honorary Chairman and Life Trustee Albert Ivar Goodman.

• Honorary President and Life Trustee Lewis Manilow.

• Life Trustees Peter C.B. Bynoe, María Bechily, Paul H. Dykstra, Carolyn McKittrick and James F. Oates.

• Women's Board Presidents Maylou Watchman, Marge Markin, Veronica O'Neill, Eileen Wells, Sondra A. Healy, Barbara Samuels, Carole David Stone, Gay Thomas, Carol Prins, Linda Hutson, Joan Coppleson, Rosemary Tourville, Susan J. Wislow, Susan D. Underwood and incoming President Alice Sabl.

There are two theater professionals whose extraordinary efforts have played a critical role in the Goodman's artistic and institutional growth for more than two decades: General Manager Katherine Murphy and Associate Producer Steve Scott.

Finally, we thank the Chicago theater audience—the greatest theater audience in the world—for making it all possible.

Thank you again to everyone, and we hope you enjoy this celebration of the Goodman Theatre.

Lester N. Coney
Chairman of the
Board of Trustees

Robert Falls
Artistic Director

Roche Schulfer
Executive Director

THE FIRST

SIXTY YEARS

July 22, 1922

On the afternoon of Thursday, July 22, 1922, the Board of Trustees of the Art Institute of Chicago convened to consider an extraordinary offer. In attendance were half a dozen trustees, among them some of the leading citizens of Chicago: Martin A. Ryerson; Potter Palmer; the architect Howard Van Doren Shaw and Robert Harshe, the director of the Institute. Board chairman Charles Hutchinson read aloud the following letter:

My Dear Mr. Hutchinson,

Much pleased to have your letter of the 23rd June expressing your appreciation of what we hope to do for the Institute in memory of Kenneth...

We are now ready to supply [the funds] under conditions mentioned and see no reason why preliminary work should not begin at once.

Very sincerely,
Mr. and Mrs. William O. Goodman

The trustees immediately accepted the Goodman's gift: $250,000 for the construction of a theater and the creation of an endowment to fund a professional repertory company and a school of drama.

And with that, the Goodman Theatre was born. In time, the Goodman, and other theaters like it, would come to rival the Broadway producers whose work filled the commercial houses that flourished throughout the country. These new theaters would replace them as the creators of what we call the "American Theater."

Kenneth Sawyer Goodman and his daughter Marjorie, 1918.

Kenneth Sawyer Goodman and the Founding of the Goodman Theatre

The Goodmans' gift to the Art Institute paid homage to their son, Kenneth Sawyer Goodman, whose tragic death from pneumonia in 1918 cut short a life filled with creative promise. Born in 1883 into a family that had amassed a fortune in the Wisconsin lumber industry, Kenneth was given all of the advantages of a scion of wealth: exposure to the fine arts at an early age, a prep school education, then admission to Princeton University. There the young Goodman pursued an early fascination with writing, winning the editorship of the campus literary magazine, *The Tiger*.

After the obligatory post-graduation tour of Europe, Goodman returned in 1908 to a Chicago immersed in a literary and theatrical renaissance. Small private theater companies (with such apt names as the New Theatre, the Little Theatre and the Chicago Theatre Society) were launching productions of works that commercial producers shunned: the innovative and controversial plays of Ibsen and

Strindberg, for example, and the social comedies of George Bernard Shaw. Although gainfully employed in his father's lumber business, the young Goodman immersed himself in this burgeoning arts community, eventually launching a drama group at the Art Institute in tandem with a new acquaintance, director/designer Thomas Wood Stevens. Goodman wrote dozens of plays, embracing all genres from spectacles and farces to earnest social dramas. His most celebrated works were co-authored with Ben Hecht, a brash young newspaperman; among their joint works, a *commedia*-style one-act entitled *The Wonder Hat* was the most popular and is still performed today.

Although Goodman's death ended his dreams of beginning a theater workshop in Chicago, his parents' bequest ensured that those dreams would be realized in grander fashion than Kenneth had ever imagined. His old friend Thomas Wood Stevens (who had become head of the theater program at Carnegie Mellon University) was brought back to Chicago to run the nearly unprecedented combination of training school and professional repertory company. With architect Shaw in charge of the design, plans were immediately made for the construction of the new theater at the corner of Monroe Street and Columbus Drive.

After nearly three years of preparation, the new Kenneth Sawyer Goodman Memorial Theatre was dedicated on October 20, 1925, with a performance of three of Goodman's one-act plays. Two nights later, the first official production of the new company premiered: John Galsworthy's

The Forest. Stevens and his company of professional actors subsequently treated theatergoers to a wide array of dramatic fare, from classics by Shakespeare and Molière to such noteworthy contemporary works as Georg Kaiser's expressionistic drama *Gas*. At the same time, an eager group of students took classes in scene design, makeup, diction and other theater arts. But despite growing audiences and critical acclaim, the theater continually operated at a deficit, causing tensions between the Art Institute board and director Stevens. The onset of the Depression only increased these conflicts and in the spring of 1930 Stevens resigned his position, telling *The New York Times* that he "was unable to reconcile [my] views regarding the repertory of an art theatre with those of the committee appointed by the Art Institute's trustees." The professional company staggered along for another season under the direction of former Stevens disciple Hubert Osbourne, but in the spring of 1931, the Art Institute board voted to discontinue the professional wing of the Goodman Theatre. The ambitious experiment had come, temporarily at least, to a halt.

The School Years

For the next thirty years, the Goodman Theatre was in effect the Goodman School of Drama, still offering a "Members' Series" of classics and contemporary plays, but now featuring all-student casts. Headed by two Russian émigrés, Maurice Gnesin and David Itkin, the training program became one of the first in America to employ the naturalistic techniques pioneered by Constantin Stanislavsky and quickly was

Robert Falls' first
Goodman production,
Sam Shepard's *Curse
of the Starving Class*
with (from left) John
Malkovich, Jack Wallace,
Jane Alderman and
Glenne Headley.
Goodman Stage 2, 1979.

(Left) A Goodman
School production of
King Lear, 1944.

(Right) Program for the
first plays presented at
the original Goodman
Theatre, 1925.

THREE PLAYS
BY
KENNETH SAWYER GOODMAN

BACK OF THE YARDS
A PLAY IN ONE ACT

Characters:

A Priest   Walton Pyre
A Police Sergeant   Russell Spindler
A Boy   Neal Caldwell
The Boy's Mother   Mary Agnes Doyle
A Girl   Eula Guy

Mrs. Connors' flat. Chicago

THE GREEN SCARF
AN ARTIFICIAL COMEDY

Characters:

A Man   Hubbard Kirkpatrick
A Woman   Ellen Lowe

A public park

THE GAME OF CHESS
A MELODRAMA

Characters:

Alexis Alexandrovitch   Howard Southgate
Boris Ivanovitch Shamrayeff   Josef Lazarovici
Constantine   Arvid Crandall
Footman   Edward Robbin

Russia, before the Revolution

The plays are produced by the Repertory Company, under the direction of
Thomas Wood Stevens and Howard Southgate.

STAFF

C. E. WILDER, *Manager*   CHARLES SCHLESINGER, *Asst. Stage Manager*
RUSSELL SPINDLER, *Stage Manager*   BARNEY OSTERTAG, *Properties*
ARVID CRANDALL, *Lighting*   LESLIE MARZOLF, *Scene Designs*
HELEN FORREST, *Costumes*

recognized as one of the premier training programs in the country. Enrollment doubled during the 1930s, and the Goodman School student body soon included a number of future greats: Karl Malden, who made his Goodman debut in 1935 under his real name, Mladen Sekulovich; future character actor Sam Wanamaker; and, in the 1940s, actors Geraldine Page, Shelley Berman, Harvey Korman and director José Quintero.

The Goodman School was bolstered by the addition of a children's theater program, providing young actors with invaluable training and many thousands of young audiences with their first exposure to the art of the theater. Founded in 1925 by writer Muriel Brown, the program was taken over in 1931 by Charlotte Chorpenning, who would become an expert in the creation of theater for young people. More than fifty of her plays were ultimately produced at the Goodman, making her the most produced playwright in the theater's history.

But by the late 1950s, both Gnesin and Itkin were in declining health, and audience interest in the Goodman Theatre was dwindling. Since critics were not invited to productions, the work of the Goodman was unknown to the vast majority of potential audiences. The School program faced declining enrollment. Gnesin died in 1957, and Itkin retired to Arizona. To replace them, the Art Institute committee chose a director who would bring renewed vitality and professionalism to the Goodman Theatre: John Reich.

Reich and Woodman

A native of Austria (where he had been a student of the legendary Max Reinhardt), John Reich came to the Goodman with impressive credentials, both academic and professional: teaching positions at Smith College and New York University; accolades for his directing work off Broadway and for CBS Television; and well-received translations of European plays. Passionate and tireless, Reich immediately set about to re-establish the Goodman Theatre's place in Chicago's cultural landscape. He scheduled a series of public talks with well-known theater experts (including Quintero, critics Henry Hewes and Walter Kerr and designer Donald Oenslager) to help lure audiences back to the Goodman. He hired Dr. Charles McGaw, a respected teacher of acting, to run the Goodman School program. And he worked with master marketer Danny Newman to fashion a publicity campaign that would place the Goodman in the public eye once again. Using as an example the European repertory companies he knew as a young man, Reich wrote: "Today the Goodman faces a greater challenge and responsibility than ever before. It ought to be regarded not only as a school...but as an art theater for the whole city..."

In his first season, Reich instituted another innovative policy: the hiring of professional guest artists to augment the student casts of productions. Beginning with Broadway leading man Donald Buka, who played the title role in Reich's production of *The Salzburg Everyman*, Reich made a concerted effort to import the best possible professional actors to add luster and depth to Goodman offerings. Such venerated stars as Morris Carnovsky, Eugenie Leontovich, Lillian Gish and James Earl Jones brought their considerable talents to the Goodman stage, and audiences and critics responded enthusiastically. By the spring of 1969, sufficient funding had been secured to establish a fully professional company at the Goodman.

Although economic pressures forced the disbanding of this resident acting company after two seasons, Goodman Mainstage productions continued to be cast with professional actors, most imported from New York. (Goodman School students appeared in Studio Theatre and Children's Theatre productions.) After Reich's retirement in 1972, William Woodman, formerly a staff director at New York's Juilliard School, assumed the role of artistic director. Well connected to the national theater scene, Woodman brought the beginnings of national attention to Goodman productions by transferring them to Philadelphia, Washington, D.C., and Broadway. He also expanded the theater's repertoire, bringing Shakespeare back to prominence while introducing to the Goodman's growing audience a host of exciting new playwrights. Top actors from New York and Los Angeles still took the major roles, but a growing number of Chicago actors were cast in Goodman productions. And during Woodman's watch, the Goodman mounted its first major African American production, Lorraine Hansberry's *To Be Young, Gifted and Black*.

In 1975, a sequence of events began that would dramatically alter the structure of the Goodman Theatre. That fall the Art Institute, citing a $200,000 deficit, announced that it would no longer fund the Goodman School of Drama. After a series of failed attempts to find a new home for the program, a deal was struck in the spring of 1978 with DePaul University, and the Goodman School of Drama became the Theatre School at DePaul. But an even more profound change had been effected the previous year when the Goodman Theatre separated itself from the Art Institute of Chicago and, under the visionary leadership of founding chairman Stanley M. Freehling, formed its own nonprofit corporation, the Chicago Theatre Group (CTG). After more than fifty years as an adjunct, the Goodman Theatre was finally an independent cultural entity.

A New Beginning: Mosher, Mamet and Schulfer
One of the first charges of the newly formed CTG board was to hire a successor to William Woodman, who returned to New York in 1978. Their logical choice was Gregory Mosher, a young Juilliard graduate who had become Woodman's assistant, then had electrified the Chicago theater community with a series of productions under the auspices of the Goodman's new experimental wing, Stage 2. Mosher's primary producing focus was on the playwright, and he brought some of the best and brightest young writers to Stage 2: director/adapter Frank Galati; Athol Fugard, whose *Siswe Banzi is Dead* was one of Stage 2's most noteworthy successes;

(Left) John Reich, Goodman artistic director from 1957 to 1972.

(Right) William Woodman assumed the artistic directorship from 1973 to 1978.

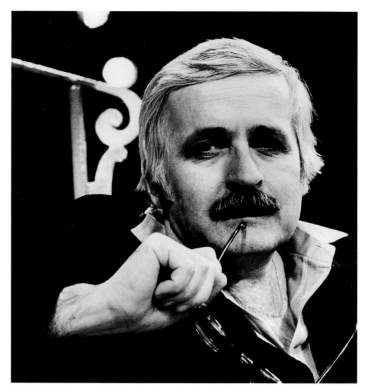

The Kenneth Sawyer Goodman Memorial Theatre as it looked in the late 1920s.

the German neo-expressionist Peter Handke; and a young actor-turned-writer who had already achieved success via an Organic Theatre production of his dark comedy *Sexual Perversity in Chicago*: David Mamet.

A Chicago native, Mamet had begun his career as an actor at Bob Sickinger's famed Hull House Theatre in the mid-1960s while also working as a busboy at Second City. Mosher's first professional association with Mamet came when the young writer, never shy about his own work, presented Mosher with a script of his latest play, proclaiming that it would be the hit of the next season. Mamet's enthusiasm was prophetic; the 1975 premiere of *American Buffalo* was a smash, establishing him as one of the major young writing talents in the country. Additional collaborations brought further success and when Mosher took on the top Goodman job he named Mamet as an associate director.

Joining Mosher and Mamet at the helm of the Goodman was an aspiring young producer, Roche Schulfer. Born and raised in the Chicago area, Schulfer began working in the Goodman box office after his graduation from the University of Notre Dame in 1973. Paired with Mosher as producer of Stage 2, Schulfer used his producing abilities to help capitalize on the artistic success of the series. In a short time, Goodman Stage 2 became a force in the off-Loop theater movement and Schulfer became a co-founder of the Off-Loop Producers' Association, later the League of Chicago Theatres. By 1980,

Schulfer had become managing director of the Goodman, the youngest manager of a major American theater company. Since then, he has continued to lead the Goodman as executive director, celebrating twenty-five years in that role in 2005; he is now recognized as one of the leading theater producers in the country.

As artistic director, Mosher continued to place the playwright at the center of the Goodman's artistic mission, producing world premiere works by established playwrights (Tennessee Williams, Edward Albee) along with plays by an unusual variety of writers from around the world: future Nobel Prize winners Wole Soyinka and Derek Walcott; British writer David Hare; and such exciting young American talents as Michael Weller, David Rabe and Richard Nelson. Mamet contributed a number of works, including new plays that would enhance his stature as the foremost playwright of his generation: *Edmond* and *Glengarry Glen Ross*, which earned the author a Pulitzer Prize and provided the Goodman with a hit Broadway transfer. Mosher and Schulfer made other innovations, too. At Schulfer's urging, in 1978 the Goodman produced a stage version of Dickens' classic tale *A Christmas Carol*; its unprecedented success and annual revivals have made it the most beloved theatrical event in Chicago theater history. Significantly greater numbers of Chicago-based artists were cast in Goodman productions, thus encouraging the growth of a theater community already becoming nationally known. Mosher and Schulfer also made a concerted effort to bring more artists and audiences of color to the

Goodman via nontraditional casting policies and such lauded productions as Soyinka's *Death and the King's Horseman*, a revival of the classic *Native Son* and an African American version of Ibsen's *An Enemy of the People*. In the spring of 1985, Mosher unveiled his New Theatre Company, a resident ensemble of artists intended to bring the work of the Goodman to a new level of excellence and professionalism. The company lasted for only a few months, but received recognition for productions of two Mamet premieres, an adaptation of Chekhov's *The Cherry Orchard* and an evening of two provocative one-acts, *The Spanish Prisoner* and *The Shawl*.

In 1985, Mosher accepted an offer too good to pass up: an appointment as artistic director at New York's famed Lincoln Center Theater. Although his departure came at a critical time for the Goodman, Mosher's seven-year directorship—with its championing of new and daring work, artistic and ethnic diversity, and new and exciting theater artists—had dramatically altered the nearly sixty-year-old institution. The Goodman was now poised to take the next step toward fulfilling the potential that its history so richly implied. All that was needed now was the next artistic leader, the visionary who would guide the Goodman into the next phase of its artistic maturity.

The Rise of the Off-Loop

By the early 1980s, a revolution had occurred in Chicago theater, fueled in part by the successes of Goodman's Stage 2. Until the late 1960s, with such exceptions as the Goodman, Second City and Hull House Theater, most local professional theater activity consisted of touring companies originating in New York. But through the 1970s, a veritable explosion of homegrown companies occurred, bringing a vitality to Chicago's cultural landscape not seen since the heyday of Kenneth Sawyer Goodman and the "little theatre" movement. On Lincoln Avenue, Kingston Mines and the Body Politic Theatre produced provocative, eclectic mixes of populist and experimental work. Stuart Gordon's Organic Theatre created explosively entertaining satires with a communal ensemble that included future stars Joe Mantegna and Dennis Franz. Victory Gardens Theater moved from a concentration on contemporary classics to an emphasis on new plays by Chicago-based writers. In Highland Park, a group of Illinois State University graduates formed the Steppenwolf Theatre, named after a popular Herman Hesse novel. The St. Nicholas Theatre (founded by Mamet, director Steven Schachter, actor William H. Macy and publicist Patricia Cox) developed a successful subscription series, a late-night series of new and experimental work, a training program (early students included John Mahoney and D. W. Moffett) and even a touring children's theater.

And on Howard Street along the Chicago/Evanston border, another young director was celebrating in 1985 his ninth season as artistic director of the much-praised Wisdom Bridge Theatre with a galvanizing, media-age interpretation of *Hamlet*. His name? Robert Falls.

ROBERT FALLS
AT THE

"I WANTED TO DO A PLAY THAT I REALLY LOVED AND THAT
I'D BEEN DYING TO DO A BIG BRECHT PLAY LIKE

GOODMAN

CHALLENGED EVERYBODY INVOLVED.
GALILEO FOR YEARS."

Making Stories Happen

Some people know from childhood what they want to spend their lives doing. Robert Falls is one of them. At a very early age he became interested in "making stories happen," creating puppet shows and live productions in Ashland, Illinois. Later, as a student at Willowbrook High School in Villa Park, he auditioned for the school's production of *Inherit the Wind*. He won a tiny role—and he was hooked. "I recall feeling as if I had found a home," he later said. "I played a photographer. My one line was 'A picture, Mr. Brady.' But on opening night, I tripped getting on stage and the line came out 'A Brady, Mr. Picture.'"

Brian Dennehy in Robert Falls' inaugural production at the Goodman Theatre, Brecht's *Galileo*.

Falls became a stalwart of Willowbrook High's theater, eventually playing Willy Loman in the school's production of *Death of a Salesman*. An omnivorous reader, he mowed through the plays in his suburban public library. And during weekend jaunts into Chicago, he witnessed the early sparks of what was to become the off-Loop theater movement.

A Career Begins

In 1972 Falls entered the University of Illinois on a playwriting scholarship from the Shubert Foundation. Eventually turning his sights to directing, he had his first major theatrical success when he staged Michael Weller's poignant Vietnam-era play, *Moonchildren,* in an old railroad depot. The show was a hit and, during Falls' senior year, Stuart Oken and Jason Brett—two University of Illinois friends who had moved to Chicago to form their own production company—called to offer him the chance to remount *Moonchildren* at the new St. Nicholas Theatre. The production earned twelve Jeff nominations, including one for Outstanding Direction

and established its young director as a force in the Chicago theater community.

After graduating in 1976, Falls went to New York briefly to study acting, then headed back to Chicago. Serendipitously, he was handed a directing slot at Wisdom Bridge, a struggling theater on Howard Street. Told he could direct any play he liked, he chose Steinbeck's *Of Mice and Men*. The production became a critical and popular success and, in the fall of 1977, Wisdom Bridge asked Falls to become its artistic director. Over the course of the next nine years, he put Wisdom Bridge on the map with a string of hits, including a stunning take on Bertolt Brecht's *Mother Courage and Her Children* (1981); a now-legendary adaptation of Jack Henry Abbott's *In the Belly of the Beast* (1983) featuring a blistering performance by William L. Petersen (later transferred to the Goodman Studio); and, in 1985, a daring pop-culture-inspired version of *Hamlet* starring Aidan Quinn. Also in 1985, Falls first worked with film actor Brian Dennehy, producing the Irish political drama *Rat in the Skull* by Ron Hutchinson. It was Dennehy's first appearance on a Chicago stage; thanks to Falls, it would not be his last.

The Next Act

Along the way, Falls further built his reputation by directing shows for a number of theaters in Chicago and New York. Among these was a dynamic production of Sam Shepard's *Curse of the Starving Class* for Goodman Stage 2 in 1979, with a powerhouse cast featuring John Malkovich, Jack Wallace, Jane Alderman and Glenne Headly.

By the mid-1980s, Robert Falls had become one of the most respected directors in Chicago. Then, at the age of thirty-one, he was chosen from a field of candidates from around the country to lead the most venerable and powerful of Chicago's not-for-profit theaters—Goodman Theatre. In the twenty years since, he has succeeded in making the Goodman one of the most important and respected theatrical institutions in the nation.

He has accomplished this by carrying out the terms he laid out to the Goodman board of directors in his first interviews. He wanted, he said, to restore the glory of the Goodman Theatre Mainstage by creating theater pieces on a grand scale, utilizing all of the Goodman's physical and financial resources to tell stories of epic size and scope. He wanted to establish ongoing collaborations with local and national artists of stature and singular vision so that the Goodman could become the home for a variety of artistic voices. He wanted to expand the repertoire of the Goodman to

reflect Chicago's increasingly multicultural landscape. And he aspired to engage all facets of that community, via productions, programs and special offerings—anything that would truly make the Goodman a theater for all Chicagoans. These tenets would form the basis of Falls' unique, dynamic approach to artistic leadership—and to an era of unprecedented success at the Goodman.

Galileo and the Inaugural Season

Officially taking the artistic reins of the Goodman in the spring of 1986, Falls immediately began to plan his inaugural season. In size, scope and range, it was to be the most ambitious Goodman season in decades, heralding in bold terms Falls' vision for the institution's future.

Falls' first production was one of the most demanding works of the past half-century: Bertolt Brecht's sprawling, challenging *Galileo*, starring his former Wisdom Bridge associate Brian Dennehy as the brilliant, doomed Renaissance scientist. For Falls, *Galileo* was the perfect choice, a play about new worlds and new beginnings that assert themselves despite massive pressures against them. As he told one interviewer, "It's a play that embraces all the elements of theater: size, humor, great humanity and intelligence, and huge potential for movement—everything's in motion. And it's a play about a new age coming."

True to his word, Falls used the enormous Goodman Mainstage masterfully, at one point even incorporating the auditorium's fabled center dome into the action as the stage literally erupted with Galileo's discoveries. It was a thrilling moment in a beautifully conceived production, and the Falls era was off to a grand start.

Later that spring, following the world premiere of Michael Weller's drama *Ghost on Fire*, Falls created a rollicking production of another of his favorite plays, Shakespeare's *The Tempest*. Alternately mysterious and violent, dreamlike and surreal, Falls' production emphasized the play's theatrical imagery. "Because many of the images in *The Tempest* relate to the theater, I wanted it to have a real looseness and hipness," he said. "I wanted a feeling of immediacy in the theater—to capture that certain magic that exists in a rehearsal room when the actors are wearing their own clothes and using random costumes and temporary props. It's sort of 'anti-magic', the sense of the actors creating it right in front of your eyes."

Theatricality was the hallmark of two other productions that first season. In January, longtime friend and newly appointed Associate Director Frank Galati unveiled his opulently theatrical fantasia *She Always Said, Pablo,* an original work spawned by Galati's longtime fascination with the writings of Gertrude Stein. Based on Stein's musings about her friendship with Pablo Picasso, *She Always Said,*

Pablo was a dizzying combination of dance, opera and Stein's own poetry, offering a moving portrait of a distinctly unique relationship.

At season's end director Michael Maggio, another of Falls' longtime colleagues, mounted a graceful, passionate interpretation of Stephen Sondheim and James Lapine's *Sunday in the Park with George*. Using Georges Seurat's classic pointillist painting "Sunday Afternoon on La Grande Jatte—1884" (which could be seen only a few feet away at the Art Institute of Chicago) as both a visual backdrop and a thematic through line, *Sunday in the Park* created a shimmering view of the often complex relationship between art, commerce and life. It was an immediate hit, both critically and with audiences, and was extended through the end of the summer of 1987. Soon after its opening, Falls appointed Maggio Associate Artistic Director.

From start to finish, the 1986–1987 season was charged with excitement and filled with epic ideas, a fitting inauguration for the three-man team now in charge. Falls summed it up this way: "It's exactly the season I wanted to do. I don't feel a compromised moment in it. It belongs to us."

Robert Falls had arrived at the Goodman and made it his own.

"A THEATER CAN'T BE A MUSEUM;

IT HAS TO BE A LABORATORY."

ROBERT FALLS

AS DIRECTOR

Creating the Play…When asked to define his own distinctive approach to the direction of plays, Robert Falls offered this assessment: "If there's any talent I have, it's an ability to plug into material emotionally. It comes from observing, watching, but it's nothing that can be taught; it's not craft."

An insatiable researcher, Falls spends months steeping himself in the world of the play prior to design meetings and casting sessions. Yet he is a consummate collaborator and early rehearsals often see the company working around the table, exploring ideas and memories related to that play's subjects and themes, spurred by Falls' infectious enthusiasm and passion. As acclaimed actress Cherry Jones once related, "With Bob I always feel I'm with a childhood playmate, very large and tall, but still wonderfully gentle." Falls' unique combination of generous collaboration and vivid conceptualism has created a series of intensely theatrical, emotionally powerful productions and has earned him a reputation as one the finest directors of his generation.

**Robert Falls
at the Goodman**

1979
*Curse of the
Starving Class*

1984
In the Belly of the Beast

1986
Orchards

Galileo

1987
The Tempest

1988
Landscape of the Body

Pal Joey

1989
The Speed of Darkness

The Misanthrope

1990
The Iceman Cometh

1991
Book of the Night

1992
On the Open Road

*Riverview: A Melodrama
with Music*

1994
The Night of the Iguana

1995
Three Sisters

1996
A Touch of the Poet

1997
*The Young Man
from Atlanta*

1998
Griller

Death of a Salesman

2001
House and *Garden*

Blue Surge

2002
*Long Day's Journey
into Night*

The Guys

Lobby Hero

2003
The Goat or, Who Is Sylvia?

2004
Finishing the Picture

Hughie

2005
Dollhouse

2006
A Life in the Theatre

King Lear

Frank's Home

A partial list of honors
Robert Falls has earned
over the course of his
Goodman Theatre leader-
ship includes the following:

2006
Tony Award nomination for
Best Play (*Shining City*)

Honorary Doctor of Fine
Arts, Lake Forest College

2003
"Number One Regional
Theater in the U.S."
(Goodman Theatre),
Time magazine

Tony Award for Best
Revival of a Play (*Long
Day's Journey into Night*)

Tony Award nomination
for Best Director of a Play
(*Long Day's Journey
into Night*)

Drama Desk Awards for
Outstanding Director of a
Play and Outstanding
Revival of a Play (*Long
Day's Journey into Night*)

Artistic Leadership Award,
League of Chicago Theatres

Election to the American
Academy of Arts and
Sciences

2002
National Broadway Theatre
Award for Best Direction of
a Touring Production (*Aida*)

2001
"Chicagoan of the Year"
Award, *Chicago* magazine

1999
Cover/Featured Artist,
American Theatre
magazine

Governor's Award for
Outstanding Contributions
by an Individual Artist,
Illinois Arts Council

"Best Productions of
the Season" (*Death
of a Salesman*),
Time magazine

Jeff Awards for Best
Direction of a Play and
Best Production (*Death of
a Salesman*)

Tony Awards for Best
Direction of a Play and
Best Revival of a Play
(*Death of a Salesman*)

1998
"Chicago Artists of the
Year" recognition,
Chicago Tribune

1997
Tony Award nomination for
Best Play (*The Young Man
from Atlanta*)

Cary Grant Artist-in-
Residence, Quad City
Arts Program

1996
Crystal Award for
Outstanding Contribution
to Chicago Theatre,
Chicago Drama League

1995
Obie Award for
Outstanding Direction
(*subUrbia*)

Tony Award nomination for
Best Revival of a Play (*The
Rose Tattoo*)

1993
"Most Powerful People in
American Theatre"
recognition, *American
Theatre* magazine

1992
Tony Award for
Outstanding Regional
Theatre (Goodman
Theatre)

"Best Productions of the
Season" (*The Iceman
Cometh*), *Time* magazine

1991
Jeff Award for Outstanding
Production (*The Iceman
Cometh*)

1988
Jeff Award for Outstanding
Direction (*Pal Joey*)

Major Works

Anthony Starke as Terry and Maggie Siff as Nora in Rebecca Gilman's *Dollhouse.*

From the outset of Robert Falls' tenure at the Goodman, his vision has been guided by a fundamental respect for both tradition and innovation. New works, he feels, should be produced with all the care and respect traditionally given to the classics, and classics should be produced as though they were written yesterday.

Over the years, Falls has treated Chicago audiences to works by Shakespeare, Williams, Miller, Molière and many others. He has crafted each production so as to unearth the contemporary within the historical. The results have been consistently surprising, fresh and theatrically dynamic.

At the same time Falls has maintained and built upon the Goodman's commitment to new plays and playwrights, forging long-term relationships with some of today's most celebrated writers—August Wilson, Edward Albee and Eric Bogosian, to name only a few—as well as some of the most vibrant new writers on the horizon. And Falls' love of the musical, that most American of theatrical forms, has resulted in some of the greatest Goodman highlights of the last two decades.

NEW LOOKS AT CLASSIC PLAYS

1987 / The Tempest
Falls' concept for his 1987 production of Shakespeare's *The Tempest* was, in his words, "based almost entirely on dreams. What our *dreams* are to our sleeping life, the *theater* is to our waking life. They're a series of images and metaphors—beautiful or horrifying or erotic or lyric—that are played out for us and that, at their best, have profound meaning. We must have dreams—and theater—to release us."

The production was indeed the stuff of dreams—and pretty spectacular dreams at that. "Robert Falls has done it again," said the *Chicago Sun-Times*. "This *Tempest* is full of divine deceptions and bewitchment."

1989 / The Misanthrope
The 1989/1990 Goodman season opened with Falls' production of Molière's *The Misanthrope*, starring stage and film actress Kim Cattrall and Chicago favorite David Darlow in the leading roles of Alceste and Celimene. Setting the play in contemporary Hollywood, Falls worked closely with adapter Neil Bartlett to revise Molière's original to reflect the Machiavellian politics of the film industry, a perfect backdrop for the play's biting social satire.

1994 / The Night of the Iguana

"It starts out as a play about sex," Robert Falls told the *Chicago Sun-Times* in March 1994. "But it ends up as a deeply poetic meditation on God and on loneliness in a godless world." Falls had long wanted to bring the beauty and redemptive power of Tennessee William's neglected classic to the stage and did so in 1994 with Cherry Jones, Chicago stage veteran-turned-film star William L. Petersen and a superlative supporting cast. The success of his production was summed up by the headline in the *Chicago Tribune* review: "What a Night!"

2005 / Dollhouse

Following the Goodman's successes with Rebecca Gilman's *Spinning into Butter*, *Boy Gets Girl* and *Blue Surge*, Robert Falls came up with a new challenge for the prolific Chicago playwright: an adaptation of Henrik Ibsen's *A Doll's House* that would move the play to a contemporary Chicago setting. Falls felt Gilman's worldview and dark sense of humor would restore the startling power of Ibsen's social commentary. The result was *Dollhouse*, an exhilaratingly contemporary view of life in the affluent class.

2006 / A Life in the Theatre

In 1977, the Goodman had presented the world premiere of David Mamet's stunning two-hander *A Life in the Theatre* and it was an immediate sensation. After a celebrated off-Broadway production in the late 1970s, the play had fallen into relative obscurity until Falls, fascinated by the heartfelt lyricism with which Mamet infused the complex central relationship, revived it as part of his 2006 festival honoring the playwright's multifaceted career. Falls' luminous production restored the play to its rightful place as an early Mamet classic.

PREMIERE WORKS

1989 / The Speed of Darkness

When he first read Steve Tesich's *The Speed of Darkness*, Falls was struck by the play's motif of secrets and betrayal, punctuated by dark humor. Opening in April 1989, his production received wide praise for a presentation that, as one critic wrote, "stripped away everything but the essentials." Tesich and Falls developed a close personal bond that led to future collaborations, including a Falls-directed Broadway production of *The Speed of Darkness* in 1991.

1992 / On the Open Road

Robert Falls continued his collaboration with Tesich in 1992. In this comic meditation on art, religion and the nature of power, *Road's* two main characters echoed the innocence and disillusionment of Beckett's archetypal tramps in *Waiting for Godot*. To create the titular road, Falls again joined forces with Soviet émigré designer George Tsypin who had created the massively theatrical settings for *Galileo* and *The Misanthrope*. *On the Open Road* enjoyed a subsequent New York run at the Public Theater.

(Above) *The Misanthrope*,
featuring David Darlow
and Kim Cattrall.

(Left) Robert Falls'
production of Shakespeare's
The Tempest.

1997 / The Young Man from Atlanta
Though Horton Foote's play had received
its world premiere in a small production
a year earlier, Falls' staging was the first
major production of the Pulitzer Prize
winner, a haunting portrait of a family's
disintegration under the weight of
long-suppressed secrets and deceptions,
featuring noted stage and screen actors
Shirley Knight and Rip Torn. Following its
Goodman run, the play moved to Broadway
where it won accolades for its stars, its
director and its revered playwright.

2001 / Blue Surge
After producing two successful Rebecca
Gilman plays, Robert Falls himself took
the helm of her next work. Although
traditional in structure, the play's uncom-
promising dissection of class conflicts
made it the center of controversy upon its
premiere in June 2001. A subsequent
New York production, featuring Falls'
direction and much of the original cast,
elicited such commentary as this in *New
York* magazine: "*Blue Surge* never cheats
and yet manages to surprise as it unfolds
with increasing intensity. The climax is
persuasive, shatteringly beautiful and
absolutely right."

MUSICALS

1988 / Pal Joey
A longtime fan of this Rodgers and Hart
classic, Falls restored the sardonic cyni-
cism of John O'Hara's original stories to
the musical's libretto and mounted a
dazzling production that featured sinewy

choreography by Broadway's Ann
Reinking. One of the most opulent
productions in Goodman history, the
show delighted audiences throughout
an extended summer run.

1991 / Book of the Night
Three years later, Robert Falls brought
Goodman audiences this urban song cycle,
penned by composer-lyricists Louis Rosen
and Thom Bishop. Told strictly in song
and dance, *Book of the Night* followed
the dusk-to-dawn wanderings of a dozen-
plus characters played by such Chicago
favorites as John Herrera and Hollis
Resnik. The result was an emotionally
complex panorama of dreams and
disappointments revealed on an urban
summer night.

*1992 / Riverview: A Melodrama
with Music*
Long fascinated with the American
melodrama of the 19th century, with its
mixture of spectacle, music and social
commentary, Falls commissioned an
update of the genre from Chicago playwright John Logan. Set in the 1940s at
Riverview Amusement Park, a legendary
North Side haunt, the show featured
popular songs from the era that com-
mented ironically on the conflicts and
prejudices revealed in the play's narrative.
The largest-scale work the Goodman had
ever produced, *Riverview* featured a cast
of nearly forty and sumptuous sets that
included an onstage roller coaster.

(Above, left) *The Speed of Darkness* by Steve Tesich, with Brigitte Bako, Andy Hirsch and Stephen Lang.

(Above, right) David Mamet's *A Life in the Theatre*, with Matt Schwader as John and David Darlow as Robert.

(Left) William L. Petersen and Paula Korologos in Tennessee Williams' *The Night of the Iguana*.

According to Falls: "The thing that I love about acting is that someone's up there going through the emotions that we suppress. Actors have this ability to tell the truth. They've decided to risk a lot."

(Opposite) *Blue Surge* by Rebecca Gilman, featuring Steve Key and Joe Forbrich.

(Below, left) *Book of the Night*, with Jim Corti, Vicki Lewis and Hollis Resnik.

(Below, right) The company of *Riverview: A Melodrama with Music.*

(Pages following) Robert Falls' production of Rodgers and Hart's *Pal Joey*, with choreography by Ann Reinking.

Falls and Dennehy

A PERFECT MATCH

Brian Dennehy in *Long Day's Journey into Night.*

Now in their third decade as collaborators, Robert Falls and Brian Dennehy have created a unique working relationship based on their abiding respect for each other's talent. As Dennehy is the first to admit, "My professional relationship with Bob is by far the most important one in my life." Together they have made a habit of tackling large-scale powerhouse plays, most notably the major works of the greatest of American poetic realists: Eugene O'Neill.

Interpreting an American Master

Falls and Dennehy's first O'Neill collaboration was the Goodman's 1990 production of the epic portrait of hope and disillusionment, *The Iceman Cometh*, with Dennehy starring as hardware salesman and pipedream-buster Theodore "Hickey" Hickman. Anchored by Falls' sensitive direction, Dennehy's bravura star turn and an ensemble that included Hope Davis, Denis O'Hare, Ernest Perry, Jr. and James Cromwell, the production's immense power was, according to one critic, "sweeping, singing, burning and wickedly funny."

In 1996, Falls and Dennehy returned to O'Neill—this time with the 1936 tale of tragic self-delusion, *A Touch of the Poet*.

Featuring Dennehy as the tyrannical Con Melody, Pamela Payton-Wright as his long-suffering wife and Jenny Bacon as his rebellious daughter, Falls' production was a shattering interpretation of one of O'Neill's most complex works.

Six years later O'Neill's masterpiece *Long Day's Journey* arrived on the Goodman stage with Dennehy as the vain, selfish patriarch James Tyrone. A play that O'Neill himself had once claimed he'd written in "tears and blood" proved to be a towering achievement for Falls and Dennehy. The Broadway remount of the production two years later featured Dennehy, Vanessa Redgrave, Phillip Seymour Hoffman and Robert Sean Leonard.

And finally, in the fall of 2004, Falls staged O'Neill's obscure, posthumously published one-act, *Hughie,* with Dennehy as the big-time talker and small-time gambler Erie Smith. Just under an hour long and with little in the way of overt dramatic action, *Hughie* was a captivating showcase for Dennehy, now playing one of O'Neill's most tragically diminished characters. The result was a brief portrait with all the power and punch of a full-length play.

The Iceman Cometh, featuring James Cromwell as Larry Slade and Brian Dennehy as Theodore "Hickey" Hickman.

Falls on Dennehy: "What I love about him is his courage at a time when most actors, at the same point in their careers, are not going to do anything scary. It's a rare thing for a director to have a guy who comes as prepared, as hungry, as ready to tackle something with all that energy and intelligence as Brian does."

(Above) Brian Dennehy and Joe Grifasi in *Hughie*.

(Left) *A Touch of the Poet*, with Pamela Payton-Wright and Brian Dennehy.

Falls and Arthur Miller

In 1997, Robert Falls picked up an old favorite play, Arthur Miller's classic study of the crumbling American dream, *Death of a Salesman*. It seemed to Falls just as timely as it ever had been. "This is about a father who loves his son so much that he passes on all the wrong values: if you're liked, if you're handsome enough, if you're charming enough—it's all about surface appearances," Falls said in an interview. "And I think that's still a lesson we see today. We live in a society which is far more disposable than ever. We're always looking for the newer—the hotter. You're going to be displaced sometime for a younger, more attractive guy than you are."

One night not long thereafter, Brian Dennehy was in town for a visit and the two men happened to be walking down the street together when Falls noted that his friend was limping, the result of knee surgery. In that moment, Falls realized that now would be the time to do *Salesman*. Dennehy had turned sixty and age was beginning to temper his enormous innate power. Preparations for the revival began almost immediately.

Eschewing the selectively realistic approach that directors had used since *Salesman's* 1949 premiere, Falls opted for an expressionistic take on the play based on Miller's own assertion that the action essentially occurs in Willie's mind. When *Death of a Salesman* opened on the Goodman Mainstage in the fall of 1998, Falls' conceptual daring received critical raves. So did the performances: Dennehy's devastating portrayal of a man on the verge of implosion, Elizabeth Franz's heartrenching turn as Willie's wife Linda, and a raft of powerful supporting performances by Kevin Anderson, Ted Koch, Howard Witt, Steve Pickering and Kate Buddeke. Audience response was overwhelming and the production began to attract notice from outside Chicago.

A number of well-known theater professionals came to see the show and two, in particular, had a deeply significant effect on what happened next. The first was the play's author, Arthur Miller, who left the performance profoundly moved. The other was the chief critic for *The New York Times*, Ben Brantley, whose opinion appeared a few days later. Headlined "A Dark New Production Illuminates 'Salesman'" and calling Dennehy's portrayal "the performance of his career," Brantley's paean ended with this tacit blessing: "The production, rumor has it, is bound for New York next year. It is hard to imagine a better way to celebrate the fiftieth anniversary of a play that, so unlike its hero, only seems to grow larger with age."

On February 10, 1999, fifty years to the day after the premiere of the original production, Robert Falls and company opened *Salesman* at Broadway's Eugene O'Neill Theatre to rave reviews. It would go on to win Tony Awards for Best Revival of a Play, Best Director (Falls), Best Principal Actor (Dennehy) and Best Featured Actress (Franz). Following its Broadway run, the production played Los Angeles, then London, bringing the Goodman international acclaim—and forging a lasting bond between Falls and Arthur Miller.

A Moving Picture

Death of a Salesman led to a second noteworthy collaboration between Falls and Miller, a dark and corrosively funny fictionalized account of an episode in Miller's turbulent marriage to Marilyn Monroe entitled *Finishing the Picture*. Though the autobiographical elements could not be denied, Miller and Falls wanted *Finishing the Picture* to move audiences past the real-life parallels to explore deeper issues: the mystique of stardom and its connection to luck, and the role of the movies in the shaping of the American Dream. That said, the play also adhered to one of Miller's career-long themes: the question of where one person's responsibility to another begins and ends. *Finishing the Picture* opened the 2004–2005 season with a star-studded cast: Stacy Keach, Matthew Modine, Scott Glenn, Linda Lavin, Frances Fisher, Stephen Lang, Harris Yulin and rising Chicago actress Heather Prete. The show drew sellout crowds and garnered international attention.

Finishing the Picture would turn out to be the playwright's final work. Miller died on February 10, 2005, at the age of eighty-nine. In a tribute to Miller written for the *Chicago Tribune*, Falls said: "He was simply and unpretentiously a writer, rolling up his sleeves and relishing his work, finding as much joy in crafting a play as he did in crafting furniture in his shop in Connecticut. As we'd watch a rehearsal, he'd lean over to me to say, 'Gee, that's a marvelous scene,' or 'Gee, that works well.' And I'd see that tremendous satisfaction that comes simply from the act of creating something."

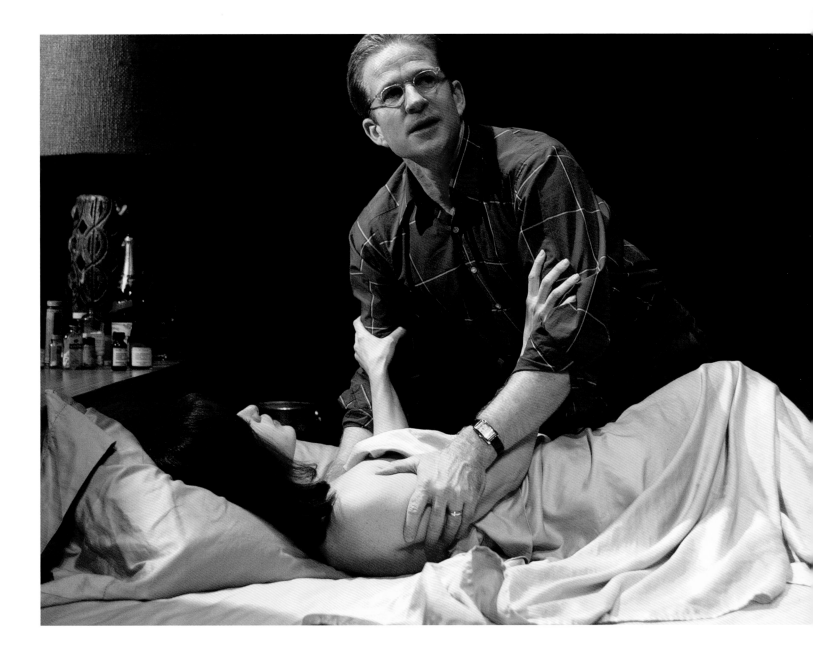

"MILLER IS TO ME
THE GIANTS.
WILLIAMS AND
THE SERIOUS PLAY

ONE OF
HE, ALONG WITH
O'NEILL, CREATED
IN AMERICA."

ROBERT FALLS

"I'M ATTRACTED TO THE GREAT EUROPEAN THEATERS

BUT WITH EACH DIRECTOR ACHIEVING THAT

THE GOODMAN: QUALITY

WHERE THERE'S A COLLABORATIVE VISION AIMED AT ONE GOAL,
GOAL IN HIS OWN WAY."

AND DIVERSITY

Building a Team: Formation of the Artistic Collective…

During his tenure at Wisdom Bridge Theatre, Robert Falls worked with Frank Galati and Michael Maggio, directors with whom he had developed great mutual respect and friendship. They shared similar backgrounds: they had grown up in the Chicago area, studied theater in college and risen steadily through the ranks of Chicago's off-Loop scene. All three had directed at the Goodman during the administrations of William Woodman and Gregory Mosher. For Falls, having both men as associates at the Goodman was imperative.

Falls based his leadership model on such institutions as the Royal Shakespeare Company and Scotland's Citizens Theater, which had thrived for twenty-five years under the shared leadership of two directors and a designer. A similar structure would allow Falls to incorporate Galati's and Maggio's unique aesthetic perspectives into the overall artistic vision of the Goodman, and would also help to alleviate the potential for burnout in the creative leadership of the theater.

Falls' strategy proved ingenious. The three longtime collaborators had great faith in each other. As Maggio put it, "You couldn't construct this kind of collaboration in a mechanical fashion. We've always been each other's biggest fans." Falls was able to provide Galati and Maggio with an artistic home and a voice in how that home would function. For the Goodman, the major benefit of the artistic leadership triumvirate—the Artistic Collective—was obvious: a guaranteed association with three of the city's top directors.

The Collective Grows… As the Goodman's success grew, so did its concerns and responsibilities. In particular, Falls realized that the three-artist Collective was only the beginning: true diversity at the Goodman could only be effected by adding more artists to its governing core, artists whose own distinctive passions and points of view would create a richer and broader-based aesthetic.

Enter David Petrarca, a young director who had made a mark in both New York and Chicago theater circles. Joining the Goodman initially as part of the TCG/NEA Directing Fellowship program for outstanding young theater practitioners, Petrarca brought a youthful energy, particularly via a reinvigorated series of productions and special events in the Goodman Studio. Falls was so impressed with Petrarca's contributions that, in 1988, he made Petrarca the fourth Goodman artistic associate.

The next and most significant phase of the Collective's expansion came in 1992—the year the Goodman took home a special Tony Award for Outstanding Regional Theatre—with the appointment of two more outstanding directors: Chuck Smith, whose decades of work in Chicago had made him the unofficial dean of the city's African American theater community; and director/writer Mary Zimmerman, a young Northwestern-trained talent whose graceful, playful adaptations of such narrative texts as

The Arabian Nights were attracting a sizable off-Loop following. Other associates—including actress/educator Cheryl Lynn Bruce and actor/director Harry Lennix—would soon join the Collective, make significant contributions to the evolution of the Goodman's diverse aesthetic, then move on to pursue careers in other performance arenas. Their effect on the increasingly varied identity of the Goodman, however, was essential.

Today's Artistic Collective (which includes actor/director Henry Godinez and triple-threat actress/playwright/director Regina Taylor, in addition to Galati, Zimmerman and Smith) is recognized by critics, audiences and theater professionals as the most accomplished of its kind in the American theater. True to his word, Robert Falls has assembled a group of artists whose collective and individual passions and standards of excellence have helped solidify the Goodman's reputation as the premier regional theater company in the United States.

Frank Galati

CHICAGO'S RENAISSANCE MAN

Called by legendary Broadway composer John Kander "a great invigorator—a man who makes you want to write," Associate Director Frank Galati has achieved near-legend status himself as an actor of power and grace, an imaginative and sensitive director, an award-winning playwright and screenwriter, and a revered professor at Northwestern University. The recipient of two Tony Awards, an Academy Award nomination and countless Jefferson Awards and other honors, Galati is widely known as an artist of passion and fierce intelligence—attributes that come packaged with his trademark gentleness and generosity. As he noted in a recent interview, "I feel I have an obligation to challenge, yes, to encourage, sure, but also to hold open my arms to make sure that no one is hurt."

A Chicago native, Galati learned his craft at Northwestern where he later became a leading proponent of the theater program now known as Performance Studies, the transformation of non-theatrical texts into stage works. One stunningly successful example of this genre was Galati's first production as Goodman Associate Director, *She Always Said, Pablo* (1987), a brilliantly theatrical glimpse into the world of Gertrude Stein and Pablo Picasso told principally through Stein's own writings. Ensuing seasons have showcased Galati's unparalleled range and immense vision, from his adaptation of (and appearance in) a "mod 1960s" reworking of Feydeau's *A Flea in Her Ear* (1988) to his direction of such varied productions as Shakespeare's *The Winter's Tale* (1990), Brecht's *The Good Person of Setzuan* (1992) and Kander and Ebb's musicalization of Dürrenmatt's classic, *The Visit* (2001).

Frank Galati's seemingly limitless powers of invention ultimately boil down to a primary love: the telling of stories. "It's a compulsion," he told *Chicago* magazine, "that is somehow like the need for water and air. I don't think it's a pathology. I think it's a necessity."

Chita Rivera and John McMartin in Kander and Ebb's *The Visit*.

Frank Galati at the Goodman			
1974 *Winnebago*	1988 *Passion Play*	1990 *The Winter's Tale*	1995 *Gertrude Stein: Each One as She May*
1985 *The Government Inspector*	*A Flea in Her Ear* *(adapter/performer)*	1992 *The Good Person of Setzuan*	2001 *The Visit*
1987 *She Always Said, Pablo*	1989 *A Funny Thing Happened on the Way to the Forum*	1993 *Cry, the Beloved Country*	

Carmen Pelton and ensemble in the "Four Saints in Three Acts" sequence in *She Always Said, Pablo*.

Frank Galati on directing: "The role of the director is to create an environment in which all members of the creative team feel comfortable to work, to try things, to fail, to take risks—and to be brave in the expression of ideas, insights and truths about the human spirit and the human condition."

Cherry Jones, Jim True
and the cast of *The Good
Person of Setzuan*.

Chita Rivera and
ensemble in *The Visit*.

Mary Zimmerman

BRILLIANT AND PRAGMATIC

Galileo Galilei, featuring John Duykers as Galileo.

"I'm really drawn to texts that have what I think of as an open quality to them, texts that can be staged in a number of ways, that could only be translated to cinematic form," reveals Goodman Theatre Manilow Resident Director Mary Zimmerman. "I feel nicely challenged by that, by how on earth to stage them."

This willingness—some might even call it an obsession—to tackle the seemingly unstageable has been a vital part of Zimmerman's artistic vision from the beginning. From her student days at Northwestern University (where she was mentored by Frank Galati) to her early collaborations with Chicago's Lookingglass Theatre, her blend of gracefully wrought imagery, anachronistic wit and sense of childlike innocence brought her critical and audience acclaim as a uniquely compelling theatrical storyteller. Joining the Goodman as an Artistic Associate in 1992, Mary unleashed her fertile imagination upon a larger canvas and a wider

audience, resulting in some of the Goodman's most beloved and unusual productions: the theatricalization of the journals of a Renaissance genius in *The Notebooks of Leonardo da Vinci* (1993, 1997); the magical exploration of Greek mythology in *The Odyssey* (1999) and the delicacy and detail of a French merchant's exotic travels in *Silk* (2005). Zimmerman's touch has brought fresh life to more traditional texts, too, most recently with her widely hailed production of Shakespeare's *Pericles* (2006).

A Tony Award winner (for 2002's *Metamorphoses*) and the recipient of a John D. and Catherine T. MacArthur Foundation "genius" grant, Zimmerman steadfastly refuses to rest on her laurels, and her focus remains remarkably pragmatic. "Theater is always an experiment—you never know until opening night," she observes. "I'm not directing for the ages. I'm directing for right now, for this space and for these people."

Mary Zimmerman at the Goodman	1993 *The Baltimore Waltz*	1995 *Journey to the West*	1999 *The Odyssey*	2005 *Silk*
	1993, 1997 *The Notebooks of Leonardo da Vinci*	1997 *Mirror of the Invisible World*	2002 *Galileo Galilei*	2006 *Pericles*
			2003 *Trojan Women*	

(Above, left) Elaine
Yuko Qualter and Ryan
Artzberger in Mary
Zimmerman's adaptation
of *Silk*.

(Above, right) Ryan
Artzberger as Pericles.

(Below) The cast of
*The Notebooks of
Leonardo da Vinci*.

(Opposite) Jenny Bacon,
Jane Cho and Christopher
Donahue in *Journey to
the West*.

(Pages following)
Christopher Donahue
and company in
The Odyssey.

Roche Schulfer on Falls' gift for collaboration: "He has been able to create an unprecedented company of associated artists—all of whom are strong people with independent visions and very strong opinions—without ever feeling threatened. He empowers artists to do their own work and relishes their success. Bob is connected to his ego, but he's connected in a very constructive way."

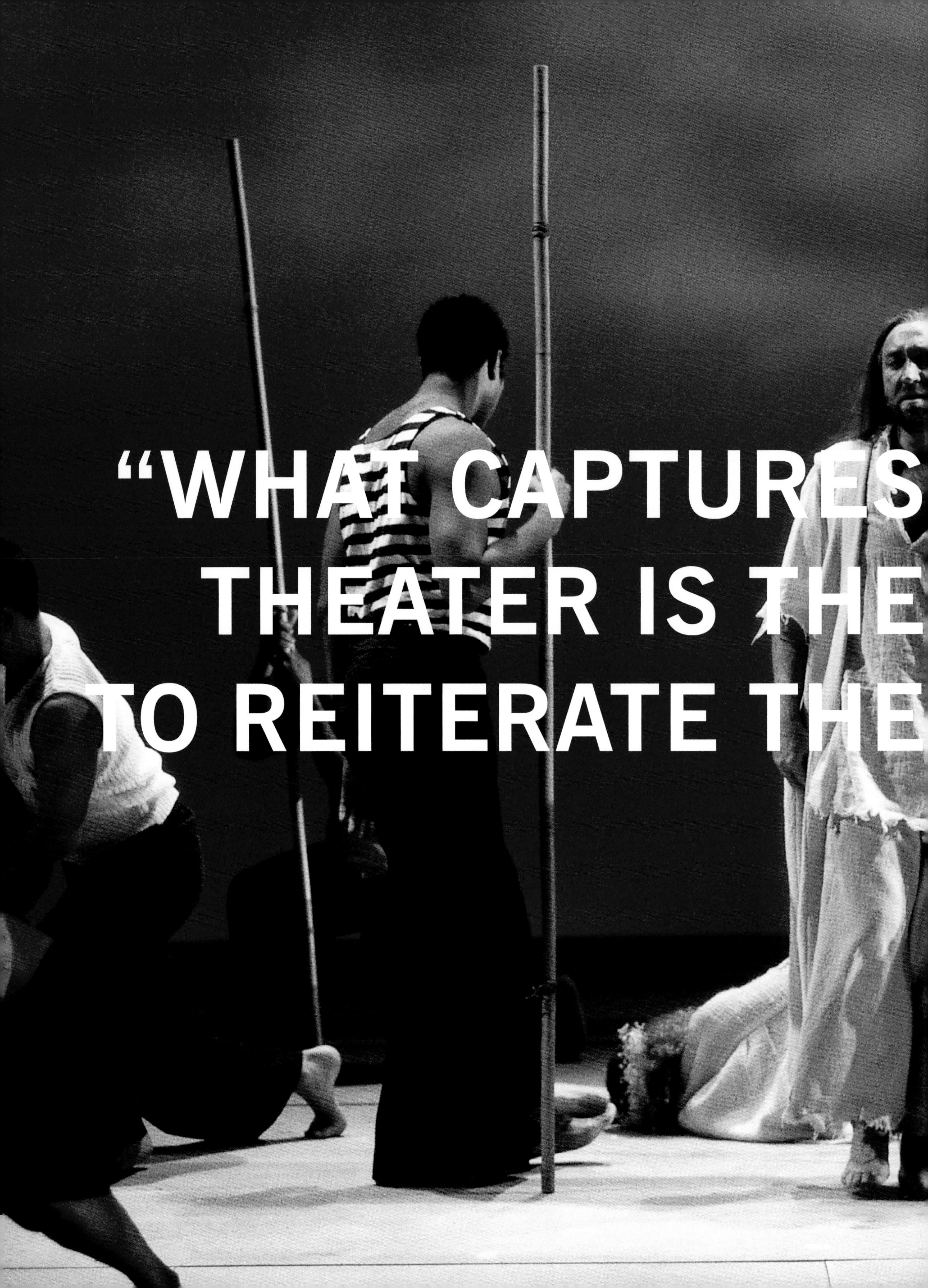

"WHAT CAPTURES
THEATER IS THE
TO REITERATE THE

PEOPLE IN THE ABSOLUTE DESIRE WORLD."

MARY ZIMMERMAN

Chuck Smith

DIRECTING AS ADVENTURE

Felicia P. Fields as Ma
Rainey in *Ma Rainey's
Black Bottom.*

Since his emergence as a theater artist in the 1970s, Goodman Resident Director Chuck Smith has created an uncommonly varied body of work. Smith got hooked on the stage by working with such famed community theaters as the Dramatic Art Guild and Experimental Black Actors Guild (X-BAG). In the winter of 1971, he was hired as an understudy for the Goodman's premiere of *The Night Thoreau Spent in Jail*—and what had started as a hobby became a profession. Smith segued from acting to directing, won acclaim with productions at such off-Loop theaters as the Chicago Theatre Company (which he co-founded) and in 1992 was invited to join the Goodman's Artistic Collective.

Over the course of his tenure at the Goodman (where he was named Resident Director in 2001), Smith has created unforgettable productions of such classics as *Ma Rainey's Black Bottom* (1997), *A Raisin in the Sun* (2000) and *The Amen Corner* (2001), working with some of Chicago's most notable acting talent: Felicia P. Fields, Ernest Perry, Jr., Harry Lennix and Irma P. Hall among many others. Well known for mentoring emerging writers, he has brought the work of Chicago playwriting talents such as Lydia Diamond, Carson Grace Becker and David Barr to Goodman audiences. His no-nonsense approach to directing has invigorated such well-known contemporary works as David Auburn's Chicago-set Pulitzer Prize winner, *Proof* (2004).

Where will Chuck Smith turn his restless sights next? In a 2003 address to the Literary Managers and Dramaturgs of the Americas, Smith concluded by quoting from August Wilson's *Gem of the Ocean:* "One of my favorite lines from the play is when Aunt Ester says, 'You are on an adventure Mr. Citizen. I bet you didn't know that. You're on an adventure and you didn't even know it.'" Added Smith with a wry, thoughtful smile, "I'll tell you one thing: I know it now."

**Chuck Smith
at the Goodman**

1989	1997	2002	2004
The Meeting	*Ma Rainey's Black Bottom*	*The Gift Horse*	*Proof*
1993–95	1998	2003	2005
A Christmas Carol	*Blues for an Alabama Sky*	*By the Music of the Spheres*	*The Story*
1995	2000	*The Death of Bessie Smith*	2006
Vivisections from a Blown Mind	*A Raisin in the Sun*		*Crumbs from the Table of Joy*
	2001		
	The Amen Corner		

Artist to artist: After seeing Chuck Smith's Goodman production of *Ma Rainey's Black Bottom*, the late August Wilson sent Smith a note. "Thank you for a beautiful production of *Ma Rainey*," Wilson wrote. "It is really fine, fine work. I haven't seen any better."

(Left) T'keyah Crystal Kemah and Harry Lennix in *A Raisin in the Sun*.

(Right) David Auburn's *Proof*, with Dwain Perry and Karen Aldridge.

(Below) Phillip Edward Van Lear in *The Amen Corner*.

Regina Taylor

CAPTURING THE MUSIC AND DRAMA OF LIFE

Caroline Clay as Gin del Sol in *Oo-Bla-Dee*.

Best known as an award-winning actress, Regina Taylor has forged a different identity among Goodman audiences: as a uniquely gifted and eloquent playwright and director. Through such divergent plays as *Oo-Bla-Dee* (1999), *Drowning Crow* (2002) and *Crowns* (2004), Taylor has created richly textured portraits of the African American experience that capture specific moments in time while exploring such universal themes as the shifting of generational values, the evanescence of our lives and the role of art in our world.

Taylor gained broad public recognition for her performance on the television series *I'll Fly Away* (1991-1993). A year later, she made her Goodman debut with a pair of intriguing one-act plays in the Goodman Studio, produced under the umbrella title *The Ties That Bind*. Earning high praise for her artful combination of poetry, ritual and shrewd contemporary insight, Taylor joined the Goodman Artistic Collective

later that year. Since then, she has challenged audiences with her provocative views of life and culture while entertaining them with her sometimes radical reinvestigations of theatrical storytelling.

Perhaps the most defining aspect of Regina Taylor's writing is her sense of musicality. As she told one interviewer, "I hear things musically. Just in terms of speech or looking at the world, there's a music, a rhythm, a heartbeat to everything. That's how I write the dialogue." This is amply illustrated in *Crowns,* a foot-stomping blend of gospel music and stories adapted from Michael Cunningham and Craig Marberry's volume of black women photographed in their elaborate church hats. We're doing the truths of their lives," Taylor said, calling the extravagantly designed headwear "wonderful windows into these women's souls." Audiences agreed, making *Crowns* one of the best attended shows in Goodman history.

Regina Taylor at the Goodman

1994	1997	2002	2006
The Ties That Bind (Playwright)	*Transformations* (Curator/Co-director)	*Drowning Crow* (Playwright)	*The Dreams of Sarah Breedlove* (Playwright/Director)
1995	1999	2004	
Escape from Paradise (Playwright/Performer)	*Oo-Bla-Dee* (Playwright/Co-director)	*Crowns* (Playwright/Director)	
	2000		
	Millennium Mambo (Curator/Co-writer/ Performer)		

Regina Taylor on the theater: "There's this wonderful leap that you take in terms of imagination and the worlds that you explore—the people that you encounter and get to know intimately beneath the skin. It's a mystical place and it's very cathartic when you go through it, when you take that journey."

Jason Delane in
Drowning Crow.

Henry Godinez

BRINGING THE WORLD TO CHICAGO

At Henry Godinez's rehearsals, the actors are typically relaxed and having a great time—because Godinez is a true actor's director. A performer himself, he's that rare combination of talent, theatrical savvy, intelligence and passion—an infectiously enthusiastic artist who has loved the theater ever since the moment he first stepped out onto an empty stage.

Cuban-born and Texas-bred, Godinez came to Chicago in the mid-1980s. Immediately recognized for his acting gifts, Godinez performed at theaters all over the city, including the Goodman, where his appearances included roles in Michael Maggio's *Romeo and Juliet* and *A Christmas Carol*.

Turning his sights to directing, Godinez founded Teatro Vista and brought the rich world of contemporary Latino writing to Chicago audiences through such productions as his 1995 rendering of José Rivera's magical-realist drama *Cloud Tectonics*, a co-production of Teatro Vista and the

Goodman. Beginning in 1996, he helmed several incarnations of *A Christmas Carol* and, the following year, he was made a member of the Goodman Artistic Collective.

In 2000, Godinez took on *Zoot Suit*, the masterwork of the "Godfather of Chicano Playwriting" Luis Valdez. Wildly theatrical, the show featured a sizzling score, athletic swing-dance numbers and a large Latino cast that attracted a new, enthusiastic Latino audience to the Goodman. To further cultivate this audience, in 2003 Godinez inaugurated the Goodman's Latino Theatre Festival, a showcase of readings and performances featuring local, national and international Latino artists. The first year was a success and the second festival (featuring Godinez's harrowing production of Luis Alfaro's *Electricidad*) was even more so. Filling a crucial gap in Chicago theater programming, the Latino Theatre Festival has added even more dimensions to Henry Godinez's remarkably multifaceted career.

Cecilia Suárez as the title character in Luis Alfaro's *Electricidad.*

Henry Godinez at the Goodman			
1995 *Cloud Tectonics*	1998 *Straight as a Line*	2000 *Millennium Mambo*	2004 *Electricidad*
1996–2001 *A Christmas Carol*	2000 *Zoot Suit*	2003, 2004, 2006 Latino Theatre Festivals	

Henry Godinez on the power of the theater: "For me, the definitive experience is being moved...provoked... motioned...challenged...changed. I leave the theater a different person than when I came in."

(Left) The "vecinas" in *Electricidad*: Sandra Delgado, Tanya Saracho, Marisabel Suarez and Laura E. Crotte.

(Right) Sandra Marques and Eric Lloyd Ambriz in Karen Zacarías' *Mariela in the Desert*.

Culture Clash (Richard
Montoya, Ric Salinas
and Herbert Siguenza)
in *Culture Clash in
AmeriCCa*.

The company of
Luis Valdez's *Zoot Suit*.

Michael Maggio (1951–2000)

MAKING SOMETHING OUT OF THE CHAOS

Phoebe Cates and
Michael Cerveris as
Romeo and Juliet.

Despite a chronic lung disease that made it virtually impossible for him to take a normal breath, Michael Maggio became one of the brightest stars of Chicago theater—a director with a winning combination of wit, imagination, passion, consummate artistry and humanity. After establishing his reputation in the late 1970s with off-Loop productions of such large-scale works as *Candide,* Maggio was hired in 1979 for his first Goodman Mainstage production, *Cyrano de Bergerac.* Following other Goodman successes and a four-year stint as artistic director of Northlight Theatre, Maggio was appointed the Goodman's Associate Artistic Director and soon after created two of his most praised productions: a luminous rendering of Stephen Sondheim's *Sunday in the Park with George* and *Romeo and Juliet,* set in post-World War I Chicago and paying homage to Maggio's own heritage. In 1991, after ill health forced him to leave a production of *A Midsummer Night's Dream,* Maggio underwent a risky double lung transplant. He celebrated its success by doing what he had always done: he went right back to work.

His "comeback" show was the stirringly beautiful musical *Wings,* the story of a former aviatrix whose life is altered by a stroke; later remounted off Broadway, it earned Maggio and star Linda Stephens coveted Obie Awards. A variety of hits followed: a vibrant rendering of Tom Stoppard's *Arcadia;* three world premieres by playwright Keith Reddin, including the

dark comedy *All the Rage,* and the first production of Rebecca Gilman's *Boy Gets Girl.* During this busy time, Maggio was also named dean of DePaul's Theatre School. Sadly, after nearly a decade of relatively good health, he developed transplant-related lymphoma and on August 19, 2000, just two months before the Goodman was to move into its new home on Dearborn Street, he died. He was forty-nine.

One of the Goodman's most prolific directors (twenty-three productions in all), Michael Maggio was also one of its most versatile. But his astonishing body of work contained a variety of common elements: a fascination with the human condition; unerring grace and intelligence; and a passionate belief in the power of the theater to illuminate and transform. Michael was a great human being and a consummate artist, and his ample spirit lives on at the Goodman Theatre.

To honor Michael's memory, the Goodman Theatre established the Michael Maggio Directing Fellowship. Granted annually to an early-career Chicago director, the fellowship provides recipients with a cash award and the valuable experience of working at the Goodman Theatre alongside some of the best directors in the business. Recipients of the award have included Lynn Ann Bernatowicz (2002–2003), Mignon McPherson (2003–2004), Ann Filmer (2004–2005) and Dado (2005–2006).

**Michael Maggio
at the Goodman**

(Opposite) Michael Maggio's production of *Sunday in the Park with George*, featuring Deanna Dunagan and Dale Morgan.

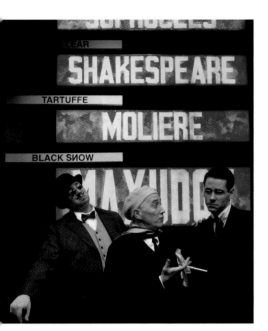

(Above, left) The cast of Keith Reddin's *Black Snow*.

(Above, right) Ora Jones and Linda Stephens in Jeffrey Lunden and Arthur Perlman's musical adaptation of *Wings*.

(Below) Mary Beth Fisher and David Adkins in Rebecca Gilman's *Boy Gets Girl*.

August Wilson (1945-2005)

THE TWENTIETH CENTURY CYCLE

Eriq LaSalle and
Roscoe Lee Browne in
Two Trains Running.

Although August Wilson was not an official member of the Goodman Collective, his twenty-year relationship with the theater was one of its most important and most influential. Beginning with *Fences* in 1986, the Goodman became the first American theater to produce all ten plays in Wilson's extraordinary cycle of works chronicling the African American experience in each decade of the twentieth century. Two of these productions were world premieres: *Seven Guitars* in 1995 and *Gem of the Ocean* in 2003. Others were pre- or post-Broadway tours (featuring such eminent Wilson interpreters as Charles S. Dutton and Roscoe Lee Browne) or vivid local productions staged by Chuck Smith (*Ma Rainey's Black Bottom,* 1997) and Jonathan Wilson (*Joe Turner's Come and Gone,* 1991).

When the new Goodman Theatre facility opened in the fall of 2000, it seemed only fitting that the first production would be an August Wilson play: *King Hedley II,*

produced here prior to its award-winning New York run.

It was fitting, too, that August Wilson would deliver the dedication address for the new theater on November 9, 2000. On that occasion, he offered his audience a fiery challenge:

The actors will walk across the stage, they will howl, they will conspire with and struggle and gain truth—the sum total of our collective experience—and hold the mirror as it were up to nature.

From this stage will be raised a ruckus and a noise that will echo in the whirlwind.

Tragically, this remarkable voice was stilled in the fall of 2005 when Wilson died of liver cancer. Passionate, sometimes combative, always provocative, August Wilson was a true poet of the theater, an observer of his world in all of its confounding, frustrating, beautiful contradictions.

**August Wilson
at the Goodman**

1986	1991	1997	2000
Fences	*Joe Turner's Come and Gone*	*Ma Rainey's Black Bottom*	*King Hedley II*
1989	1992	1999	2003
The Piano Lesson	*Two Trains Running*	*Jitney*	*Gem of the Ocean*
	1995		2007
	Seven Guitars		*Radio Golf*

(Left) Mary Alice
and James Earl Jones
in *Fences*.

(Above) *Joe Turner's
Come and Gone*, with
Norman Matlock, Dick
Sasso and Pat Bowie.

Michole Briana White
and Russell Hornsby in
August Wilson's *Jitney*.

Gem of the Ocean, featuring Greta Oglesby as Aunt Ester and Yvette Ganier as Black Mary.

(RIght) S. Epatha Merkerson in *The Piano Lesson*.

(Pages following) Leslie Uggams and Charles Brown in *King Hedley II*.

"YOUR
TO WRESTLE WITH
WILL CAUSE
ANGELS

WILLINGNESS
YOUR DEMONS
YOUR
TO SING."

AUGUST WILSON

New Voices, New Visions…"The directors who stay in our memory are those who have had some ability to capture perfectly the times they are in," Robert Falls once said in an interview. "It's the same for playwrights. It has to do with somehow being true to yourself within a certain awareness of pop culture—the melding of art with an ability to synthesize what is going on currently."

This philosophy is clearly embodied in a burgeoning group of contemporary playwrights, directors, performers and designers whose work has been brought to life on the Goodman's stages. Over the years this roster has included writers such as Scott McPherson, Rebecca Gilman, Charles Smith and Adam Guettel—a diverse collection of talents linked by their ability to tap directly into the zeitgeist. These new voices are encouraged through extensive commissioning and play development programs, an annual New Stages Festival and ongoing alliances with other theaters around the nation.

The Goodman also attracts the most exciting directors, both established and up-and-coming. Over the years, the theater has collaborated with such renowned visionaries as Harold Prince, JoAnne Akalaitis, Lee Breuer and Peter Sellars while offering opportunities to a new generation of artists including David Petrarca and Kate Whoriskey.

Outstanding performers have found a home at the Goodman and audiences have been transported by the work of a dazzling array of acting talents from Chicago and around the world. The artistry of the designer is on constant display at the Goodman, with established visionaries and imaginative new creators bringing their magic to Goodman productions.

The Playwrights

REBECCA GILMAN

In the late 1990s Robert Falls was given a copy of *The Glory of Living,* written by a young Chicago scribe named Rebecca Gilman. The play's raw honesty made an instant fan of Falls, and soon thereafter he offered Gilman a commission to write a new play for the Goodman. She responded with *Spinning into Butter,* a clear-eyed look at institutionalized racism on the campus of a small New England college. Produced at the end of the 1998–1999 season, the show's controversial run was extended three times and broke a Goodman box office record for the most tickets sold in a single day.

Butter's success led to Gilman's second Goodman commission, *Boy Gets Girl,* which premiered on the Goodman Mainstage in the spring of 2000 under the direction of Michael Maggio. Alternately hilarious and harrowing, the play details the systematic destruction of a young woman's life by an insistent stalker. As with *Spinning into Butter,* the central character was brought to forceful life by actress Mary Beth Fisher. The Goodman's success with *Boy Gets Girl* led to a noteworthy run at New York's Manhattan Theatre Club and Rebecca Gilman quickly became one of the most produced playwrights in the country.

Falls himself directed Gilman's next two Goodman productions. The first, a corrosive study of American class tensions entitled

James Leaming, Robert Breuler, Mary Beth Fisher and Mary Anne Thebus in *Spinning into Butter.*

Blue Surge, also enjoyed a subsequent transfer, this time to the Public Theater in New York. More recently, Falls and Gilman collaborated on *Dollhouse,* an audacious reimagining of Ibsen's classic set in Chicago's Lincoln Park neighborhood in 2005. Laced with Gilman's trademark ironic satire and brutal humor, *Dollhouse* provided a sleekly disturbing view of the clash between upward mobility and disintegrating American values.

SCOTT MCPHERSON

One of the most successful shows ever to find its way onto the Goodman stage was Scott McPherson's touching drama *Marvin's Room* in 1990. McPherson, a respected Chicago actor as well as a gifted writer, drew from his own experiences with illness to create a tender, intimate play about healing and family.

When the Goodman offered to produce the world premiere of *Marvin's Room,* McPherson had had only one other play produced, a comedy entitled *'Til the Fat Lady Sings,* at Chicago's off-Loop Lifeline Theatre. He had written the first draft of *Marvin's Room* while working at a warehouse in the Chicago suburb of Schaumburg. He admitted in an interview years later that "I wrote a lot of it when I was out there, which is why I was eventually fired. I wrote this play on the back of their commission reports."

Though not explicitly about AIDS, *Marvin's Room* was written at the apex of the AIDS crisis and it struck a deep chord. It concerns a woman who has spent much of her life devoted to the caretaking of others before learning that she herself has leukemia. But far from being somber, *Marvin's Room* is full of quirky humor and warmth of spirit. McPherson managed to find a tone for the play—absurdism shot through with compassion—that was perfectly suited to the times.

Directed by Artistic Associate David Petrarca (who would direct every major production of the play thereafter), *Marvin's Room* was a phenomenal success at the Goodman and went on to be produced off Broadway in 1992, winning McPherson both a Drama Desk Award and the Outer Critics Circle Award for Best New Play. Three years after a Goodman remount in 1993, the play was made into a major motion picture starring Meryl Streep and Diane Keaton. But McPherson, who also penned the screenplay, didn't live long enough to see the finished film. He died from complications of AIDS in 1992 at the age of thirty-three.

ADAM GUETTEL

Called "a composer for the new century" by the *Los Angeles Times*, Adam Guettel is one of the American musical theater's most vital new voices. He comes by this talent naturally: he is the grandson of composer Richard Rodgers and the son of Mary Rodgers who created the 1950s classic *Once Upon a Mattress*. But far beyond this exceptional pedigree, Adam Guettel has managed to find a style that is all his own.

The Goodman's first association with Guettel came in 1999 with a production of *Floyd Collins*, a collaboration with Tina Landau for which Guettel wrote the music and lyrics. Based on the true story of a young Kentucky man whose entrapment in a cave led to America's first media circus, Guettel and Landau's multilayered portrait of people whose dreams fail to come true enthralled Goodman audiences. Five years later, in association with Seattle's Intiman Theatre Company, the Goodman premiered Guettel's *The Light in the Piazza*, a story of love and unexpected romance. With a book by playwright Craig Lucas and filled with Guettel's glorious songs, the production not only won Chicago acclaim but also paved the way for a New York transfer. Guettel subsequently won a 2005 Tony Award for Best Original Score, one of six Tony honors accorded the production.

STEPHEN SONDHEIM

Renowned composer and lyricist Stephen Sondheim developed an ongoing alliance with the Goodman Theatre through hit revivals of *Sunday in the Park with George* (1986) and *A Little Night Music* (1994). The 2002–2003 season featured that rarity, a new Sondheim musical. With libretto by John Weidman, *Bounce* detailed the boom-or-bust lives of the famed Mizner brothers and their circle, brought to life by some of the country's finest musical performers: Richard Kind, Howard McGillin, Michele Pawk and screen legend Jane Powell. Directed by Hal Prince, *Bounce* ran for the summer at the Goodman, then transferred to Washington's Kennedy Center for an extended run.

Laura Esterman and Lee Guthrie in the original production of *Marvin's Room*.

CHARLES SMITH

One of the most compelling Goodman-commissioned new works was Charles Smith's epic *Black Star Line.* Premiering in the winter of 1996, Smith's historical drama focused on the life and times of one of America's most controversial African American leaders: Marcus Garvey, founder of the late 19th century "Back to Africa" movement. Told in vividly theatrical terms (and masterfully directed by Tazewell Thompson), *Black Star Line* ignited a renewed debate among Chicago's African American leaders about the wisdom of Garvey's philosophy and caused lively discussions among Goodman audiences. It also brought much-deserved praise to its playwright, who had already built a local reputation for his historically-based analyses of American society.

LESLIE ARDEN

Director David Petrarca's award-winning 1996 staging of *The House of Martin Guerre* introduced audiences to a stunning new musical talent, Leslie Arden. A native of Canada, Arden created a haunting score

and a compelling book (co-written with Anna Theresa Cascio) for this new version of a centuries-old tale of love, betrayal and eventual violence set in the countryside of sixteenth century France.

KIA CORTHRON

Over the course of the last fifteen years, Kia Corthron's distinctive theatrical voice has brought her to a position of prominence in the American theater. Robert Falls, an early admirer of Corthron's work, commissioned her to write *Seeking the Genesis,* a politically-charged drama about institutionalized racism in education, social services and the United States at large. Boosted by an award from the Kennedy Center for New American Plays, *Seeking the Genesis* received its world premiere in the Goodman Studio in November 1996 with an outstanding Chicago cast featuring Ora Jones. It went on to receive a production off Broadway at Manhattan Theatre Club the following year. Wrote one critic: "The playwright has found that rare marriage of real life and theatrical poetry."

(Opposite) *The House of Martin Guerre*, with Julain Molnar and Willie Malnati.

(Above, left) Howard McGillin, Jane Powell and Richard Kind in *Bounce*.

(Above, right) *Seeking the Genesis*, with Demetrius D. Thornton, Ora Jones and Raphael Vargas Chestang.

(Left) The cast of *Black Star Line*.

The Directors

JOANNE AKALAITIS

JoAnne Akalaitis has, over the course of her career, inspired admiration and controversy. Her bold work has often been categorized as "avant-garde" or "postmodern," bringing her a reputation as one of America's most daring directors. In 1990, Akalaitis brought her unique style to the Goodman with an in-your-face staging of John Ford's bloody Jacobean classic *'Tis Pity She's a Whore*, which featured a bevy of the nation's brightest young actors: Lauren Tom, Jesse Borrego, Joan Cusack and Don Cheadle. Highly visual and laced with references to fascist Italy in the 1930s, Akalaitis' take on Ford's classic intrigued, delighted and confounded audiences.

LEE BREUER

In 1990, Robert Falls invited Lee Breuer, a major force in America's avant-garde theater movement, to bring his masterwork, *The Gospel at Colonus*, to the Goodman. A retelling of Sophocles' *Oedipus at Colonus* that melded Greek drama and African American church service, *Gospel* featured a cast of more than sixty singers and actors, including legendary groups such as The Soul Stirrers, The Five Blind Boys of Alabama and Chicago's own Roebuck "Pops" Staples. The joyous result thrilled Goodman audiences and critics alike.

HAROLD PRINCE

The legendary Hal Prince has directed twice at the Goodman, most recently the Stephen Sondheim musical *Bounce* in 2003. A year earlier, Prince had joined forces with another legend, Carol Burnett, whose *Hollywood Arms* was a thinly veiled autobiography of her own complex family history. Co-authored with daughter Carrie Hamilton (who tragically died of cancer in the early phases of production), *Hollywood Arms* featured dynamite performances by Linda Lavin, Frank Wood and Michele Pawk, who won a Tony for her work in the Broadway transfer production.

PETER SELLARS

Known for his audacious reimaginings of classic texts, director Peter Sellars provided the Goodman with perhaps its most controversial production: his 1995 staging of Shakespeare's *The Merchant of Venice*. Set in modern-day California on a stage adorned only with tables and video monitors—and featuring a multiracial cast—Sellars' production emphasized the moral and spiritual bankruptcy of a world too conscious of economic status. Audiences were polarized and ticket sales soared. A subsequent tour brought Sellars' confrontational production to audiences in London, Paris and Hamburg.

DAVID PETRARCA

One of the most prolific directors in the Goodman's history, David Petrarca has created several of its most acclaimed productions. His first show after joining the Artistic Collective in 1988 was a triumph: the world premiere of Sally Nemeth's *Mill Fire*, a wrenching tale of a tightly knit community ripped apart by tragedy. Two years later, he guided Scott McPherson's touching drama *Marvin's Room* to its debut in the Goodman Studio, then helmed each of its subsequent major productions until its premieres in New York and London. Obviously at home with new work, Petrarca proved to be equally surefooted with the classics, offering fresh interpretations of works by Thornton Wilder and Friedrich Dürrenmatt. His 1994 postmodern rendering of Shakespeare's *Richard II* was a highlight, featuring a powerfully nuanced performance by Jeffrey Hutchinson as the titular king.

Petrarca is equally skilled with musicals, as he proved with his triumphant premiere of Leslie Arden's *The House of Martin Guerre*. And his talent for comedy was abundantly clear in his productions of Moss Hart's *Light Up the Sky* and Amy Freed's *The Beard of Avon*, each a delightful dissection of the world of the theater.

Petrarca's Goodman successes eventually brought him offers from New York theater producers and the worlds of television and film; after a fifteen-year association with the Artistic Collective, he left the Goodman in 2004 to pursue his burgeoning freelance career. He left behind him one of the most eclectic and extensive bodies of work of any director in the theater's history and a legacy as one of the most dynamic of the Goodman's resident artists.

KATE WHORISKEY

In 2002, young director Kate Whoriskey brought her idiosyncratic visual and performance style to the Goodman with a blistering production of *Drowning Crow*, Regina Taylor's revisionist adaptation of Chekhov's *The Seagull*. A year later she was back with a vividly romantic revival of Tennessee Williams' 1951 comedy *The Rose Tattoo*. With actors John Ortiz and Alyssa Bresnahan, Whoriskey created a strangely seductive comic world that drew audiences in and held them fast. Whoriskey continued her relationship with the Goodman in 2004 with her darkly comic interpretation of George Bernard Shaw's *Heartbreak House*, bringing a surrealistic aura to Shaw's portrait of a world on the brink of war.

(Above, left) Peter Sellars' production of *The Merchant of Venice*.

(Above, right) Ora Jones and Greg Vinkler in David Petrarca's production of *The Beard of Avon*.

(Below, left) Linda Lavin in *Hollywood Arms* by Carrie Hamilton and Carol Burnett, directed by Harold Prince.

(Below, right) Lauren Tom and Jesse Borrego in JoAnne Akalaitis' production of *'Tis Pity She's a Whore*.

(Pages following) Derek McLane's set design for Kate Whoriskey's production of *The Rose Tattoo*, with John Ortiz as Alvaro Mangiacavello.

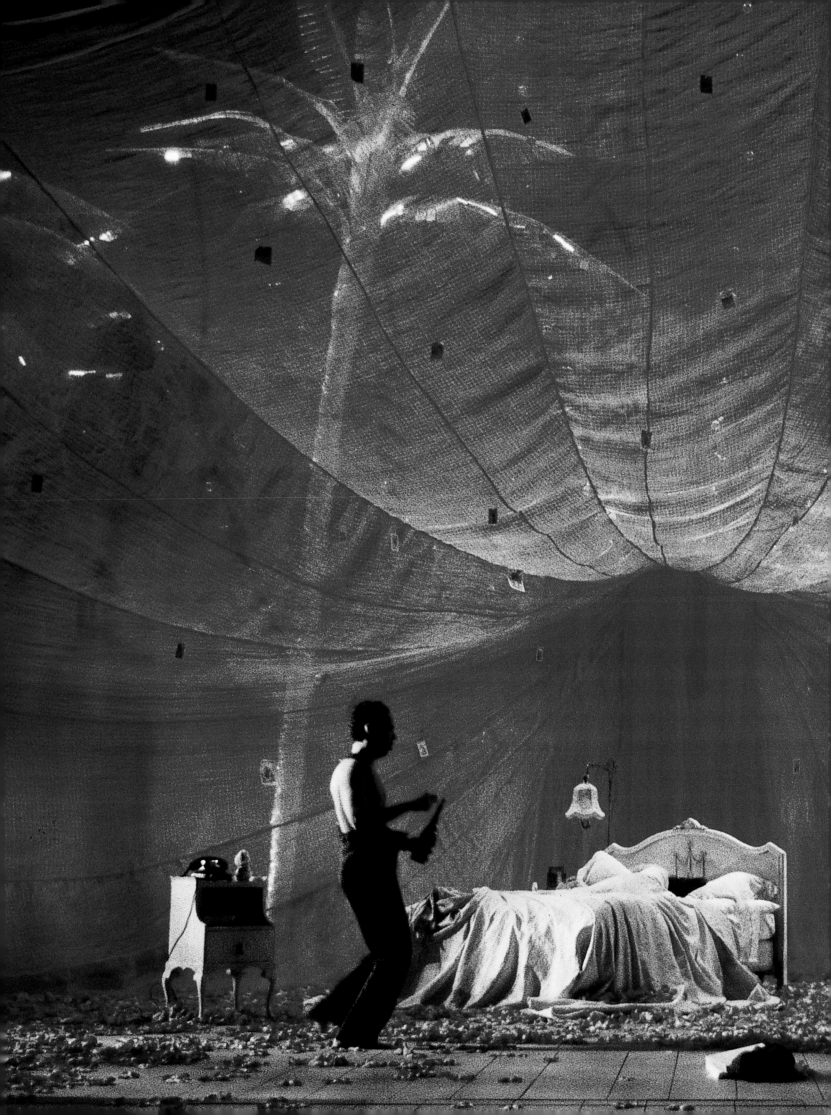

The Actors

Since 1986 audiences have seen scores of outstanding performers and performances on the Goodman Theatre's stages, with a number of actors making regular appearances in Goodman productions. Following are just a few of the many outstanding performing artists who have contributed to the Goodman's most recent two decades of success:

Stephen Lang in
Beyond Glory.

DAVID CALE

A Goodman favorite since the late 1980s, David Cale has created a memorable body of vivid solo performances and characters in such pieces as *Lillian* and *Floyd and Clea Under the Western Sky.*

PATRICK CLEAR

The epitome of the guy-next-door, Patrick Clear has brought low-key charm to a variety of modern and classic plays including Sarah Ruhl's *The Clean House* and Edward Albee's *The Goat or, Who Is Sylvia?*

MATT DECARO

Matt DeCaro's Goodman career has embraced serious works by Rebecca Gilman and Edward Albee, as well as the outrageous farce of David Mamet's *Romance.*

CHRISTOPHER DONAHUE

A longtime collaborator with Mary Zimmerman, Christopher Donahue has used his authoritative presence and poetic range to anchor Zimmerman's interpretations of *The Odyssey, Journey to the West* and *Silk.*

FELICIA P. FIELDS

Now a Broadway fixture, Felicia P. Fields has brought her infectious humor and incomparable song stylings to a variety of productions, most memorably *Ma Rainey's Black Bottom.*

MARY BETH FISHER

From a wise-cracking ice queen in *Light Up the Sky* to an uptight physician in *The Clean House*, Mary Beth Fisher's remarkable range has also been evident in her memorable collaborations with Rebecca Gilman.

SPALDING GRAY

For nearly twenty years, Spalding Gray shared with Goodman audiences his unique blend of humor, storytelling and self-analysis in such solo performances as *Morning, Noon and Night* and *Monster in a Box.*

ORA JONES

From her debut in *A Christmas Carol*, Ora Jones has created dynamic characters with a trademark intelligence and humor, most recently the elder sister in *Proof*.

STEPHEN LANG

Stephen Lang's passionate intensity has electrified a number of Goodman productions including *The Speed of Darkness*, *Finishing the Picture* and his recent solo tribute to Congressional Medal of Honor recipients, *Beyond Glory*.

HARRY LENNIX

Before he became a television and film mainstay, Harry Lennix created indelible stage characters in such lauded productions as *Ma Rainey's Black Bottom* and *A Raisin in the Sun*.

SANDRA MARQUES

Sandra Marques has won audience and critical acclaim for her no-nonsense approach to a variety of characters, including the very different mothers of *Electricidad* and *Mariela in the Desert*.

WILLIAM J. NORRIS

The original Ebenezer Scrooge, William J. Norris has brought his flinty mixture of intelligence and passion to a vast number of roles and shows, including *Cry, the Beloved Country*.

ERNEST PERRY, JR

The longest Goodman acting resume belongs to Ernest Perry, Jr., who made his debut in 1979; it includes celebrated performances in Cheryl West's *Puddin' n Pete* and Regina Taylor's *Oo-Bla-Dee*.

STEVE PICKERING

Steve Pickering has played everything from Puck, in Michael Maggio's *A Midsummer Night's Dream*, to Howard, Willy Loman's nemesis in *Death of a Salesman*, to Kent, in Fall's most recent production, *King Lear*.

BARBARA ROBERTSON

Equally at home in musicals (including Falls' revival of *Pal Joey*), comedy or drama, Barbara Robertson most recently appeared as the wronged wife in *The Goat or, Who Is Sylvia?*

JACQUELINE WILLIAMS

Jacqueline Williams' forceful intelligence has been displayed in Chuck Smith's production of *The Story* and Robert Falls' *The Young Man from Atlanta*, among many others.

HOWARD WITT

A graduate of the Goodman School of Drama, Howard Witt has appeared in everything from Chekhov to Mamet, and returned most recently as The Fool in *King Lear*. He received a Tony nomination for his memorable Charlie in *Death of a Salesman*.

(Left) Spalding Gray.

(Below, left) David Cale in *Floyd and Clea Under the Western Sky.*

(Below, center) William J. Norris in *Cry, the Beloved Country.*

(Below, right) Barbara Robertson in *The Goat or, Who is Sylvia?*

(Opposite) Sandra Marques in *Electricidad*.

(Left) Christopher Donahue in *The Odyssey*.

(Right) Mary Beth Fisher in *The Clean House*.

(Below, left) Howard Witt in *Boy Gets Girl*.

(Below, right) Jacqueline Williams in *The Story*.

(Left) Patrick Clear in *The Goat or, Who Is Sylvia?*

(Below, left) Ora Jones in *Proof.*

(Below, right) Harry Lennix in *Ma Rainey's Black Bottom.*

(Left) Felicia P. Fields in *Ma Rainey's Black Bottom.*   (Right) Matt DeCaro in *Romance.*   (Below) Ernest Perry, Jr. in *Oo-Bla-Dee.*

The Designers

The art of theatrical design is a complex one, requiring both unbridled imagination and clear-eyed practicality. In the past two decades, Goodman audiences have been treated to dozens of indelible theatrical images created by the greatest artists now working in the American theater. What follows is a representative sampling of the incomparable designers who have brought their visions to the Goodman's stages:

SANTO LOQUASTO

Perhaps best know for his film work, Loquasto has created memorably towering environments for such Robert Falls productions as *Three Sisters* (for which he also designed costumes) and *Long Day's Journey into Night*.

JAMES F. INGALLS

One of the acknowledged masters of lighting design, Ingalls has brought his subtly dramatic touch to Goodman musicals (*The House of Martin Guerre*), classics (*Three Sisters, The Merchant of Venice*) and premieres (*Dollhouse*).

MARK WENDLAND

Wendland's detailed, expressionistic stage designs have won wide acclaim, most notably for Falls' productions of *Death of a Salesman* and *A Life in the Theatre*.

MICHAEL PHILIPPI

Equally at home with lighting or scenic design, Philippi has designed a wide range of Goodman productions including *The Goat or, Who Is Sylvia?, Death of a Salesman* and *A Life in the Theatre*.

BIRGIT RATTENBORG WISE

A resident artisan at the Goodman, costume designer Wise is a consistent collaborator with Goodman directors Robert Falls, Chuck Smith and Kate Whoriskey.

DANIEL OSTLING, MARA BLUMENFELD, AND T. J. GERCKENS

Although each of these designers enjoys a thriving career, Ostling (sets), Blumenfeld (costumes) and Gerckens (lights) are most widely known for their ongoing collaboration with director Mary Zimmerman.

ROBERT CHRISTEN

The Goodman's longtime resident lighting designer, Christen has amassed a resume that includes such incandescent successes as *Sunday in the Park with George, Marvin's Room* and every production of *A Christmas Carol* since its 1978 premiere.

(Opposite) *Silk* (2005): Set design by Daniel Ostling, costume design by Mara Blumenfeld, lighting design by T.J. Gerckens.

(Following pages) *Three Sisters* (1995): Set and costume design by Santo Loquasto, lighting design by James F. Ingalls.

(Opposite) *Sunday in the Park with George* (1987): Set design by John Lee Beatty, costume design by Nan Cibula, lighting design by Robert Christen.

A Life in the Theatre (2006): Set design by Mark Wendland, costume design by Birgit Rattenborg Wise, lighting design by Michael Philippi.

THE GOODMAN:

COMMUNITY

Widening the Reach

When Robert Falls became artistic director in 1986, he did more than expand the varieties of theater art that were to be produced on the Goodman's stages. He also insisted that the Goodman reinvigorate its programming efforts to reach a wider, more diverse audience. Part of this objective, of course, he achieved by expanding and diversifying the Goodman's artistic mission to include productions accessible to a wider cross-section of Chicago's population. But in addition, Falls brought with him a passionate dedication to the city's students and educators, encouraging the creation of educational and community-based programs that currently bring the theater experience directly into the lives of thousands of young Chicagoans.

Students fill the Albert Theatre for a Student Subscription Series matinee performance.

Such programs had been part of the Goodman's mission since its earliest days. In the late 1920s, Thomas Wood Stevens and director Whitford Kane inaugurated the Goodman Theatre Amateur Drama League play festival, which hosted work by dozens of small theaters in the area, including in 1930, a production of *Julius Caesar* from the progressive Todd School in Woodstock featuring a magnetic fifteen-year-old named Orson Welles. Through the ensuing decades, classes, student matinees and other forms of outreach were offered periodically and the Goodman Children's Theatre made theater fans of tens of thousands of youthful audience members. Goodman education programs received a bigger boost in 1979 with the creation of a department of education and community programs. In addition to student performances and internships for college-aged pre-professionals, the department conducted outreach activities at such unconventional sites as the University of Illinois' Bowman Center for the Elderly and Joliet's Stateville Penitentiary.

What Falls had in mind was a deeper, richer experience for students, one that would show teenagers the limitless possibilities for theatrical expression. And unlike theaters that created special, sometimes watered-down attractions for high school audiences, the Goodman should, according to Falls, make its best work available along with workshops and materials for teachers that encouraged the study of Goodman productions in classes beyond the standard English and drama curricula. Using these guidelines, Falls and his staff created a program that would soon be emulated by theaters throughout America: the Goodman Student Subscription Series. Beginning with the 1986 production of *Galileo*, special matinee performances of Goodman shows were presented (free of charge, thanks to the largesse of a number of corporate and foundation sponsors) for selected classrooms from Chicago public high schools, each of which would be able to see *all* of the Goodman Mainstage productions produced during that school year. Students and teachers also would receive individual copies of scripts, special teacher and student guides to each production, classroom visits from Goodman staff and artists and, eventually, video documentaries that offered students a guided tour of the making of Goodman productions. Students also would participate in lively discussions after each matinee performance, exchanging ideas and opinions with the artists they had just seen onstage.

The Series was an immediate hit—teachers and students were thrilled to have access to the same productions as regular Goodman audiences, and Goodman actors marveled at the intelligent, enthusiastic reception they received from the well-prepared student audiences. Such challenging productions as *The Iceman Cometh* and Peter Sellars' unconventional *The Merchant of Venice* received rapturous responses from student viewers; the demand for tickets from parents of student participants became so great that a separate Parent's Program was established to encourage family participation in Goodman productions.

Now entering its third decade, the Student Subscription Series has formed the nucleus for a variety of comprehensive programs for Chicago's young people. The power of theatrical performance has been carried into a number of Chicago neighborhoods, for example, in the form of workshops that allow young artists to create and perform their own stage works. The first of these programs was the Young People's Drama

Workshop, established in the early 1990s at the Dearborn Homes, one of the city's more progressive public housing developments. Formed in collaboration with the Chicago Housing Authority, the program was run by noted Chicago actress and teacher Cheryl Lynn Bruce, a member of the Goodman Artistic Collective from 1998 to 2004. Under Bruce's enthusiastic guidance, neighborhood children aged eight to seventeen participated in acting and movement classes, built scenery and costumes, and presented a new production each summer to sold-out audiences. A similar program was created by Resident Artistic Associate Henry Godinez at Pilsen's Mexican Fine Arts Center Museum. Called the "Yollocalli Program" because of its association with the museum's junior division, this six-week immersion in performance and visual arts has given scores of Latino young people their first taste of participation in theater and has spawned the professional careers of several young participants.

The newest of these programs, the Goodman General Theater Studies (GTS) program, brings together young people from a variety of communities, using the Goodman Theatre itself as a resource and performance laboratory. The GTS program provides an intensive series of workshops in all phases of dramatic performance, including acting, directing, playwriting and stage management. Students also see a variety of theater work, from productions at the Goodman to shows at some of the city's most experimental small venues. The GTS final showcase is a comprehensive presentation of student design portfolios and performances.

Few Goodman programs are as important to the life of the theater itself as the Goodman Professional Internship Program. Each season, approximately forty college students and recent college graduates begin their professional careers as Goodman interns, working in such areas as stage management, casting and production. This on-the-job training provides the Goodman with a fresh influx of energy and ideas every four months, and gives its recipients comprehensive exposure to and experience in the day-to-day world of professional theater. The program's results are impressive: former Goodman interns can be found in major staff positions in a score of regional theaters (including the Goodman) as well as in major public relations firms, film production companies and commercial theaters on and off Broadway.

A Christmas Carol: From Generation to Generation

Another long-term Goodman tradition has consistently succeeded in delighting children and adults alike. Since its first production in 1978, *A Christmas Carol* has played to well over a million audience members, becoming the most beloved production in a now-crowded Chicago holiday performance lineup.

Its success, however, wasn't assured. Prior to the Goodman's production, only one other regional theater, the Guthrie in Minneapolis, had mounted the show. The size and scope of the Goodman's original production made *A Christmas Carol* one of the riskiest, most ambitious undertakings in the theater's history. Using the Guthrie's adaptation (by dramaturg Barbara Field), director Tony Mockus and set designer Joe Nieminski created a colorful, ingeniously mechanized physical production. Mockus cast more than twenty of Chicago's best actors plus a bevy of child performers. As the irascible, miserly Ebenezer Scrooge, Mockus chose William J. Norris, known primarily for his work as a member of Chicago's famed Organic Theatre. The response to the production from both critics and audiences was rapturous, prompting artistic director Gregory Mosher and general manager Roche Schulfer to schedule an encore production a year later. Audiences grew, as did the demand for subsequent revivals. Within a few years, *A Christmas Carol* had taken its place alongside the Marshall Field's windows and *The Nutcracker* as a bona fide Chicago holiday tradition.

Since 1978, seven different directors have brought their own visions to the production and five actors have succeeded Norris as Scrooge (Frank Galati, Tom Mula, Rick Snyder, William Brown and Jonathan Weir). After experimenting with a number of different adaptations of the story, the theater commissioned a version from Goodman dramaturg Tom Creamer that has been used since 1989. After playing its final performance in the old Goodman Theatre on December 30, 2000, *A Christmas Carol* moved to the new Goodman the following fall in an elaborately redesigned physical production by Todd Rosenthal. The popularity of the show has never faltered and *A Christmas Carol* is now being seen by the children and grandchildren of those original audiences from the 1970s.

Falls on the theater: "I think theater has to compete with a lot of things; therefore, it has to do things no other form can do. I think people come to the theater because people are, by and large, spiritual beings and the theater is this homemade, handcrafted event—that sort of live experience that has to become something larger, more religious."

What accounts for this success? There is the tale itself, a compelling blend of ghost story, romance, holiday cheer and redemption that grows increasingly relevant in a society prone to value economics instead of humanity. In addition, the production is scrupulously maintained and improved to avoid the staleness that sometimes infects long-running shows. The show's theme of inclusivity is another drawing card. Since the program's inception, the Goodman has made special efforts to cast a broad range of actors in the play, reflecting the breadth of Chicago's diverse community and underscoring the message of open-hearted generosity that lies at the heart of Dickens' story.

A Christmas Carol has become the first theater-going experience for thousands of children and is an annual family ritual. At any *Christmas Carol* performance one can hear a parent telling her children about the first time she encountered Marley's ghost as a child in the Goodman audience, or family groups gleefully comparing the current year's edition of the show to its predecessors. The music, the dance, the awe-inspiring effects accompanying the arrivals of the ghosts, the antics of Scrooge as he rediscovers the joy of Christmas Day—all are compelling magnets for young audiences, giving them the kind of thrilling experience that can only happen in a live theater performance. Perhaps more than any other single production, the Goodman's *A Christmas Carol* embodies the three cornerstones that Robert Falls and his collaborators aspired to achieve for twenty years and that will guide the Goodman into the future: a

striving for artistic quality onstage and off, a commitment to diversity and a dedication to bringing the work of the theater to the entire Chicago community.

From the Old to the New: The Building of the New Goodman Theatre

By the time Robert Falls began his tenure as artistic director in 1986, the Goodman Theatre building at the corner of Monroe Street and Columbus Drive had become outmoded. Because of various building restrictions, architect Howard Van Doren Shaw had been forced in the early 1920s to design a theater that was uncommonly wide and deep, with a generous but rather low proscenium opening that was ideal for presentational plays by Brecht or Shakespeare but less workable for more intimate comedies and dramas. More critically, the theater had to be built without a fly tower, which severely limited the ways in which scenery could be changed. The wide aisles of the Mainstage auditorium allowed for plenty of audience comfort, but tended to increase the separation between the audience and the onstage action, both physically and psychologically. And finally, there were the acoustic problems that had plagued the Goodman from its first production. After the theater's opening night, critic Charles Collins in the *Evening Post* noted, "Lobby conversation between the acts brought out the fact that here and there in the audience dismay and bewilderment prevailed because the dialogue could not be clearly heard...Under the dome in the center of the ceiling there seemed to be a particularly blank spot." Just prior to Falls' arrival, managing director Roche Schulfer

(Opposite, left) The 2005 production of *A Christmas Carol,* with John Lister as Marley and William Brown as Scrooge.

(Opposite, right) The original 1978 production, with William J. Norris as Scrooge and J. Pat Miller as the Ghost of Christmas Past.

commissioned a report from an acoustical engineering firm that evaluated the facility. The conclusion? If the Goodman board and staff wanted to make a long-term commitment to a facility, "we advise that your time and money would be better spent on another facility" than on the existing theater, an opinion echoed the next year by a more extensive analysis from Theatre Projects Consultants.

With these studies in hand, Irving J. Markin, the Goodman's new board chairman, began to convince the theater's trustees of the need for a new Goodman Theatre. He argued that the board had made a major investment in Falls, Galati and Maggio, and that this first-rate artistic team needed a facility to match its ambitions. Talk then turned to possible locations: the Blackstone Theater (later purchased by the Theatre School at DePaul and renamed the Merle Reskin Theatre), the Fine Arts Building, the Shubert Theatre, Navy Pier or the Civic Theatre in the Chicago Opera House. But the board and staff members entrusted with this decision kept returning to a different, more centrally located site: the old Harris and Selwyn Theatres, located on North Dearborn Street between Randolph and Lake Streets, in the heart of what had once been the busiest entertainment district in the country outside of New York's Broadway. Opened in 1922, the two playhouses had hosted scores of distinguished touring productions before their conversion into movie houses and subsequent decline into abandoned disrepair. The restoration of the theaters had been discussed since the mid-1970s, when a commission headed by

visionary cultural activist Lewis Manilow published its North Loop Theatre Study, which envisioned a performing arts center in the two theaters that would anchor the ambitious North Loop Redevelopment Plan. Both the study and the plan had been put on ice, but the 1989 election of Mayor Richard J. Daley brought both plans back into focus.

One of Daley's central concerns was the revival of the Loop as a cultural and residential center, and he envisioned a Randolph Street theater district that would draw thousands of audience members nightly to the downtown area. Along with restorations of such downtown houses as the Oriental, Chicago and Palace theaters, Daley championed the restoration of the Selwyn and Harris, preferably by an established institution such as the Goodman. With the city's blessing, the Goodman began a feasibility study of the site, addressing the challenge of fitting the theater's operations onto a relatively small footprint. Initially, the challenge seemed impossible; but working with the city, the Goodman was able to negotiate the sale of an additional site to the south of the two theaters, a plot that had contained the old Woods Theatre before it was torn down to enable the construction of the Garrick Garage. With this additional real estate, planning for the new Goodman could now begin.

Robert Falls, Michael Maggio and Frank Galati spent months touring dozens of theaters around the world to collect ideas, and their recommendations led to the ultimate design of the new spaces. In early 1995 the firm of Kuwabara, Payne,

(Above) The new Goodman takes shape: the Albert Theatre under construction, viewed from the stage left wing area of the stage.

(Left) An aerial shot of the early phase of construction, viewed from the top of the parking lot across Dearborn Street from the site.

"THIS BUILDING AND AN INVITATION ARTISTS ACROSS

IS A CHALLENGE
TO THEATER
AMERICA."

AUGUST WILSON, SPEAKING AT THE
DEDICATION OF THE NEW GOODMAN THEATRE,
NOVEMBER 9, 2000

McKenna and Blumberg, designers of many North American theaters, was chosen by the trustees and consultants, along with DLK Associates. There would be two theaters in the complex: an 850-seat proscenium theater and a three-tiered courtyard theater (inspired by the Cottlesloe Theatre in London's Royal National Theatre complex) that allowed 350 patrons to view plays set in a variety of configurations—from proscenium to in-the-round. Both theaters would have amenities for artists and audiences lacking in the old Goodman: a seventy-five-foot fly tower in the large space, vastly improved acoustics and a greater sense of intimacy. Furthermore, the complex would have ample lobby, concession, office and rehearsal space for patrons and staff. The Theatre Planning Committee was formed, led by trustee Peter C.B. Bynoe, who oversaw lead architect Tom Payne, Theatre Projects Consultants, Mesirow Stein Real Estate, McHugh Construction and the Goodman staff to insure that the new facility would be completed to meet time and budget requirements.

Meanwhile, financing for the project had started. As part of Mayor Richard Daley's North Loop Theatre District initiative, the City of Chicago played a leadership role in providing $18.8 million of Tax Increment Financing (TIF) funds for the project, which had an estimated cost of $46 million. This led to encouraging initial support from the Goodman trustees and the funding community. In addition, the Illinois Development Finance Authority made financing available while the fund-raising campaign continued.

The campaign goal, however, was large and a significant shortfall emerged in the projections. Genuine concern arose about the viability of the plan to build a new Goodman Theatre. At this critical moment, a member of the Goodman family stepped forward: Albert Ivar Goodman. Mr. Goodman (whose grandfather, Robert Barber Goodman, was the founder of the "selective logging" concept and a cousin of Kenneth Sawyer Goodman) and his mother, theater lover and patron Edith-Marie Appleton, made an extraordinarily generous gift to the Goodman that enabled the design and construction of the new facility to proceed. Their generosity, however, did not stop with the opening of the new theater. Albert Ivar Goodman and his mother's foundation (Mrs. Appleton passed away in 1999) continue to provide generous and critical support to each Goodman Theatre season. Their ongoing dedication to the Goodman is, in a word, extraordinary.

The story of the campaign is truly remarkable. From 1995 to 2000, $33.5 million was raised in the campaign for the new Goodman Theatre, enabling the $46 million project to be completed, as promised, on time and on budget. The dedication and vision of campaign co-chairs Irving Markin and Lewis Manilow, with board chairpersons James E. Annable, Sondra A. Healy and Deborah A. Bricker, was unparalled, resulting in generous support by trustees, individuals, foundations, corporations and government agencies that made the new Goodman Theatre a reality. On April 28, 1998, Mayor Daley and Goodman trustee leaders presided over the groundbreaking for the new Goodman Theater. Two-and-a-half years later the building was opened to the public, bringing to a close more than a decade of intensive work by Goodman trustees, artists and staff. On Friday, October 20, 2000 (seventy-five years to the day after the dedication of the first Goodman Theatre), staff members moved across town to the spacious new Goodman facility. For everyone connected to the Goodman, this was an especially auspicious occasion; the new building was not only a tribute to the considerable artistic successes that the Goodman had enjoyed over the past fifteen seasons, but it also pointed the way to even greater triumphs in the future. At the theater's official dedication on November 9, 2000, longtime Goodman collaborator August Wilson gave eloquent voice to the hopes, dreams and visions symbolized by this new Goodman Theatre:

Long after you and I have spent our last night of the universe, footsteps will echo across this stage and, in a language that is universal, will announce their presence with song and surety. Embodied in them will be the duty of remembrance and celebration. The duty of exploration and preservation...We are prepared to answer the call to our duty and step forward with the bold and imaginative work of which we know we are capable and to which the American Theater, with its long fruitful history, deserves.

EXECUTIVE DIRECTOR

Roche Schulfer

Roche Edward Schulfer has served as executive director of Goodman Theatre since 1980, during which time the Goodman has received numerous awards for excellence including the Tony Award for Outstanding Regional Theatre and recognition as the Best Regional Theater in the U.S. by *Time* magazine. He has been honored for his work by the City of Chicago, the *Chicago Tribune* and *Chicago* magazine, among others. He has served in leadership positions with the League of Chicago Theatres, the American Arts Alliance, the Illinois Arts Alliance, the League of Resident Theatres and Theatre Communications Group.

ARTISTIC ASSOCIATES

Frank Galati

In addition to his numerous Goodman Theatre credits, Frank Galati has received a Tony Award for his direction of *The Grapes of Wrath* on Broadway, an Academy Award nomination for his screenplay for *The Accidental Tourist* and nine Joseph Jefferson Awards. In 2001 he was inducted into the American Academy of Arts and Sciences.

Mary Zimmerman

Mary Zimmerman won the 2002 Tony Award for her direction of *Metamorphoses*, and has received ten Joseph Jefferson Awards for her work as an adapter and director. Her works have been seen at the McCarter Theatre, Berkeley Repertory Theatre, the Brooklyn Academy of Music and London's Barbican Center, among others.

Chuck Smith

A winner of both the Paul Robeson Award and the Black Theatre Alliance's Award of Merit, Chuck Smith was named a "Chicagoan of the Year" by the *Chicago Tribune* in 2001. Inducted in 2003 into the Literary Hall of Fame at Chicago State University's Gwendolyn Brooks Center, he is the editor of *Seven Black Plays*, published by Northwestern University Press.

Regina Taylor

Regina Taylor was awarded the 2000 American Theatre Critics/Steinberg New Play Award for *Oo-Bla-Dee*. As an actress, she received an NAACP Image Award and a Golden Globe Award for her television series *I'll Fly Away*. She currently appears on the CBS television series *The Unit*, created by David Mamet.

Henry Godinez

Henry Godinez has directed at regional theaters across the country including Portland Center Stage, Missouri Repertory Theatre, the Colorado Shakespeare Festival and the Signature Theatre in New York. He is the recipient of the 1999 Theatre Communications Group Alan Schneider Directing Award, as well as the Distinguished Service Award from Lawyers for the Creative Arts.

PRODUCTION HISTORY

1986–87 SEASON

Mainstage

Galileo
By: Bertolt Brecht
Translated by: Adrian Hall
& James Scheville
Directed by: Robert Falls

A Christmas Carol
By: Charles Dickens
Adapted by: Larry Sloan
Directed by: Sandra Grand

Ghost on Fire
By: Michael Weller
Directed by: Les Waters

She Always Said, Pablo
Adapted from the writings
of: Gertrude Stein
Adapted and Directed
by: Frank Galati

The Tempest
By: William Shakespeare
Directed by: Robert Falls

*Sunday in the Park
with George*
Music/Lyrics by:
Stephen Sondheim
Book by: James Lapine
Directed by: Michael
Maggio

1987–88 SEASON

Mainstage

Red Noses
By: Peter Barnes
Directed by: Jeff Steitzer

A Christmas Carol
By: Charles Dickens
Adapted by: Larry Sloan
Directed by: Michael
Maggio

Passion Play
By: Peter Nichols
Directed by: Frank Galati

Landscape of the Body
By: John Guare
Directed by: Robert Falls

A Flea in Her Ear
By: Georges Feydeau
Adapted by: Frank Galati
Directed by: Michael
Maggio

Pal Joey
Book by: John O'Hara
Music by: Richard Rodgers
Lyrics by: Lorenz Hart
Directed by: Robert Falls

Goodman Solo Series
in the Studio

The Red Throats
Written and Performed
by: David Cale

Avner The Eccentric

*Stuff as Dreams Are
Made On*
Written and Performed
by: Fred Curchack

1988–89 SEASON

Mainstage

Romeo and Juliet
By: William Shakespeare
Directed by: Michael
Maggio

A Christmas Carol
By: Charles Dickens
Adapted by: Larry Sloan
Directed by: Michael
Maggio

The Piano Lesson
By: August Wilson
Directed by: Lloyd
Richards

The Rover
By: Aphra Behn
Adapted by: John Barton
Directed by: Kyle Donnelly

The Speed of Darkness
By: Steve Tesich
Directed by: Robert Falls

*A Funny Thing
Happened On The
Way To The Forum*
Book by: Burt Shevelove
& Larry Gelbart
Music and Lyrics by:
Stephen Sondheim
Directed by: Frank Galati

Studio

Smooch Music
Written and Performed by:
David Cale

P.S. 122 Field Trips

Mill Fire
By: Sally Nemeth
Directed by: David
Petrarca

1989–90 SEASON

Mainstage

The Misanthrope
By: Molière
Adapted by: Neil Bartlett
Directed by: Robert Falls

A Christmas Carol
By: Charles Dickens
Adapted by: Tom Creamer
Directed by: Steve Scott

The Winter's Tale
By: William Shakespeare
Directed by: Frank Galati

'Tis Pity She's A Whore
By: John Ford
Directed by: JoAnne
Akalaitis

Uncle Vanya
By: Anton Chekhov
Adapted by: David Mamet
Directed by: Michael
Maggio

The Gospel at Colonus
Adapted and Directed by:
Lee Breuer
Music by: Bob Telson
Lyrics by: Bob Telson and
Lee Breuer

Studio

The Meeting
By: Jeff Stetson
Directed by: Chuck Smith

Marvin's Room
By: Scott McPherson
Directed by: David
Petrarca

Eliot Loves
By: Jules Feiffer
Directed by: Mike Nichols

1990–91 SEASON

Mainstage

The Iceman Cometh
By: Eugene O'Neill
Directed by: Robert Falls

A Christmas Carol
By: Charles Dickens
Adapted by: Tom Creamer
Directed by: Steve Scott

*Joe Turner's Come
and Gone*
By: August Wilson
Directed by: Jonathan
Wilson

*A Midsummer
Night's Dream*
By: William Shakespeare
Directed by: Michael
Maggio & Steve Scott

The Visit
By: Friedrich Dürrenmatt
Adapted by: Maurice
Valency
Directed by: David
Petrarca

Book of the Night
Music and Lyrics by:
Louis Rosen & Thom
Bishop
Directed by: Robert Falls

Studio

*Monster in a Box/
Terrors of Pleasure*
Written and Performed
by: Spalding Gray
Directed by: Renee
Shafransky

Deep in a Dream of You
By: David Cale
Directed by: David
Petrarca

1991–92 SEASON

Mainstage

Miss Evers' Boys
By: David Feldshuh
Directed by: Kenny Leon

A Christmas Carol
By: Charles Dickens
Adapted by: Tom Creamer
Directed by: Steve Scott

Twelfth Night
By: William Shakespeare
Directed by: Neil Bartlett

On the Open Road
By: Steve Tesich
Directed by: Robert Falls

*The Good Person
of Setzuan*
By: Bertolt Brecht
Translated by:
Sheldon Patinkin
Directed by: Frank Galati

*Riverview: A Melodrama
with Music*
By: John Logan
Directed by: Robert Falls

Studio

Down the Shore
By: Tom Donaghy
Directed by: David
Petrarca

Home and Away
Written and Performed
by: Kevin Kling
Directed by: Steven Dietz

Spunk
By: Zora Neale Hurston
Adapted by: George C. Wolfe
Directed by: Donald Douglass

At Briar Street Theatre

Spic-O-Rama: A Dysfunctional Comedy
Written and Performed by: John Leguizamo
Directed by: Peter Askin

1992–93 SEASON

Mainstage

The Skin of Our Teeth
By: Thornton Wilder
Directed by: David Petrarca

A Christmas Carol
By: Charles Dickens
Adapted by: Tom Creamer
Directed by: Steve Scott

Two Trains Running
By: August Wilson
Directed by: Lloyd Richards

Marvin's Room
By: Scott McPherson
Directed by: David Petrarca

Black Snow
By: Keith Reddin
(adapted from the novel by Mikhail Bulgakov)
Directed by: Michael Maggio

Cry, The Beloved Country
By: Frank Galati (from the novel by Alan Paton)
Music by: Kurt Weill
Lyrics by: Maxwell Anderson
Directed by: Frank Galati

Studio

Wings
Based on the play by: Arthur Kopit
Book/Lyrics by: Arthur Perlman
Music by: Jeffrey Lunden
Directed by: Michael Maggio

Puddin 'n Pete
By: Cheryl L. West
Directed by: Gilbert Wadadazaf McCauley

The Baltimore Waltz
By: Paula Vogel
Directed by: Mary Zimmerman

Special Event:

The Pain of the Macho
Written and Performed by: Rick Najera
Directed by: John Bowab

1993–94 SEASON

Mainstage

Dancing at Lughnasa
By: Brian Friel
Directed by: Kyle Donnelly

A Christmas Carol
By: Charles Dickens
Adapted by: Tom Creamer
Directed by: Chuck Smith

Richard II
By: William Shakespeare
Directed by: David Petrarca

The Night of the Iguana
By: Tennessee Williams
Directed by: Robert Falls

I Am a Man
By: OyamO
Directed by: Marion McClinton

A Little Night Music
Music and Lyrics by: Stephen Sondheim
Book by: Hugh Wheeler
Directed by: Michael Maggio

Studio

The Notebooks of Leonardo da Vinci
Adapted and Directed by: Mary Zimmerman

Brutality of Fact
By: Keith Reddin
Directed by: Michael Maggio

The Ties That Bind: Watermelon Rinds/Inside the Belly of the Beast
By: Regina Taylor
Directed by: Shirley Jo Finney

Solo Series

Gray's Anatomy
Written and Performed by: Spalding Gray
Directed by: Renee Shafransky

Somebody Else's Home
Written and Performed by: David Cale
Directed by: David Petrarca

The State I'm In: A Travelogue
Written and Performed by: Paula Killen
Directed by: Curt Columbus

1994–95 SEASON

Mainstage

The Merchant of Venice
By: William Shakespeare
Directed by: Peter Sellars

A Christmas Carol
By: Charles Dickens
Adapted by: Tom Creamer
Directed by: Chuck Smith

Seven Guitars
By: August Wilson
Directed by: Walter Dallas

Three Sisters
By: Anton Chekhov
Adapted by: Richard Nelson
Directed by: Robert Falls

Journey to the West
Adapted and Directed by: Mary Zimmerman

Another Midsummer Night
Music by: Jeffrey Lunden
Book/Lyrics by: Arthur Perlman
Directed by: Michael Maggio

Studio

Sin
By: Wendy MacLeod
Directed by: David Petrarca

Gertrude Stein: Each One as She May
Adapted and Directed by: Frank Galati

Vivisections from the Blown Mind
By: Alonzo D. Lamont, Jr.
Directed by: Chuck Smith

1995–96 SEASON

Mainstage

All's Well That Ends Well
By: William Shakespeare
Directed by: Mary Zimmerman

A Christmas Carol
By: Charles Dickens
Adapted by: Tom Creamer
Directed by: Chuck Smith

Black Star Line
By: Charles Smith
Directed by: Tazewell Thompson

Arcadia
By: Tom Stoppard
Directed by: Michael Maggio

A Touch of the Poet
By: Eugene O'Neill
Directed by: Robert Falls

The House of Martin Guerre
Music and Lyrics by: Leslie Arden
Book by: Leslie Arden & Anna Theresa Cascio
Directed by: David Petrarca

Studio

Cloud Tectonics
By: José Rivera
Directed by: Henry Godinez

Escape from Paradise
By: Regina Taylor
Directed by: Shirley Jo Finney

Unjustifiable Acts
By: Aaron Iverson
Directed by: Harry J. Lennix

A Pirate's Lullaby
By: Jessica Litwak
Directed by: Susan V. Booth

1996–97 SEASON

Mainstage

Randy Newman's Faust
Music and Lyrics by: Randy Newman
Book by: Randy Newman & David Mamet
Directed by: Michael Greif

A Christmas Carol
By: Charles Dickens
Adapted by: Tom Creamer
Directed by: Henry Godinez

The Young Man from Atlanta
By: Horton Foote
Directed by: Robert Falls

Light up the Sky
By: Moss Hart
Directed by: David Petrarca

All the Rage
By: Keith Reddin
Directed by: Michael Maggio

Ma Rainey's Black Bottom
By: August Wilson
Directed by: Chuck Smith

Studio

Seeking the Genesis
By: Kia Corthron
Directed by: Walter Dallas

Transformations
Conceived by: Regina Taylor

Prophecy
By: Peter Handke
Directed by: Marianne Kim

The Owl Answers
By: Adrienne Kennedy
Directed by: Susan V. Booth

Dr. Kheal
By: Maria Irene Fornes
Directed by: Regina Taylor

Red Cross
By: Sam Shepard
Directed by: Henry Godinez

The One
By: Oliver Pitcher
Directed by: Cheryl Lynn Bruce

Mirror of the Invisible World
Adapted and Directed by: Mary Zimmerman

Special Events

It's a Slippery Slope
Written and Performed by: Spalding Gray

1997–98 SEASON

Mainstage

As You Like It
By: William Shakespeare
Directed by: Michael
Maggio

A Christmas Carol
By: Charles Dickens
Adapted by: Tom Creamer
Directed by: Henry
Godinez

Griller
By: Eric Bogosian
Directed by: Robert Falls

Blues for an Alabama Sky
By: Pearl Cleage
Directed by: Chuck Smith

Design for Living
By: Noel Coward
Directed by: David
Petrarca

Play On!
By: Cheryl L. West
Music by: Duke Ellington
Directed by: Sheldon Epps

Studio

Lillian
Written and Performed
by: David Cale
Directed by: Joe Mantello

*The Notebooks of
Leonardo da Vinci*
Adapted and Directed by:
Mary Zimmerman

Let Me Live
By: OyamO
Directed by: Ron OJ Parson

1998–99 SEASON

Mainstage

Death of a Salesman
By: Arthur Miller
Directed by: Robert Falls

A Christmas Carol
By: Charles Dickens
Adapted by: Tom Creamer
Directed by: Henry
Godinez

Waiting for Godot
By: Samuel Beckett
Directed by: Michael
Maggio

Oo-Bla-Dee
By: Regina Taylor
Directed by: Regina Taylor
& Susan V. Booth

Floyd Collins
Music and Lyrics by:
Adam Guettel
Book by: Tina Landau
Directed by: Tina Landau

Jitney
By: August Wilson
Directed by:
Marion McClinton

Studio

Straight as a Line
By: Luis Alfaro
Directed by: Henry
Godinez

*Jacob Marley's
Christmas Carol*
By: Tom Mula
Directed by: Steve Scott

*Krapp's Last Tape /
Eh Joe / That Time*
By: Samuel Beckett
Directed by: Rick Cluchey
& Michael Maggio

Spinning into Butter
By: Rebecca Gilman
Directed by: Les Waters

1999–2000 SEASON

Mainstage

The Odyssey
By: Homer
Adapted and Directed by:
Mary Zimmerman

A Christmas Carol
By: Charles Dickens
Adapted by: Tom Creamer
Directed by: Henry
Godinez

*A Moon for the
Misbegotten*
By: Eugene O'Neill
Directed by: Daniel
Sullivan

Boy Gets Girl
By: Rebecca Gilman
Directed by: Michael
Maggio

A Raisin in the Sun
By: Lorraine Hansberry
Directed by: Chuck Smith

Zoot Suit
By: Luis Valdez
Directed by: Henry
Godinez

Studio

*Jacob Marley's
Christmas Carol*
By: Tom Mula
Directed by: Steve Scott

Millennium Mambo
Curated and Performed
by: Regina Taylor
By: Kia Corthron, Adrienne
Kennedy, Suzan-Lori
Parks, Ntozake Shange
& Regina Taylor
Directed by: Henry
Godinez

Schoolgirl Figure
By: Wendy MacLeod
Directed by: David
Petrarca

Special Event:

Morning, Noon and Night
Written and Performed by:
Spalding Gray

2000–01 SEASON
*Inaugural Season in the
New Goodman Building*

Albert Theatre

King Hedley II
By: August Wilson
Directed by: Marion
McClinton

A Christmas Carol
By: Charles Dickens
Adapted by: Tom Creamer
Directed by: Henry
Godinez

House
By: Alan Ayckbourn
Directed by: Robert Falls

The Amen Corner
By: James Baldwin
Directed by: Chuck Smith

Wit
By: Margaret Edson
Directed by: Steve Scott

Blue Surge
By: Rebecca Gilman
Directed by: Robert Falls

Owen Theatre

Garden
By: Alan Ayckbourn
Directed by: Robert Falls

Among the Thugs
By: Tom Szentgyorgi
Directed by: Kate Buckley

2001–02 SEASON

Albert Theatre

The Visit
Adapted from the play by:
Friedrich Dürrenmatt
Translated by:
Maurice Valency
Book by: Terrence McNally
Music by: John Kander
Lyrics by: Fred Ebb
Directed by: Frank Galati

A Christmas Carol
By: Charles Dickens
Adapted by: Tom Creamer
Directed by: Henry
Godinez

Drowning Crow
An Adaptation of Anton
Chekhov's *The Seagull*
By: Regina Taylor
Directed by: Kate
Whoriskey

*Long Day's Journey
into Night*
By: Eugene O'Neill
Directed by: Robert Falls

Hollywood Arms
By: Carrie Hamilton
& Carol Burnett
Directed by: Harold Prince

Galileo Galilei
Libretto By:
Mary Zimmerman,
Philip Glass
& Arnold Weinstein
Music by: Philip Glass
Directed by: Mary
Zimmerman

Owen Theatre

Big Love
By: Charles L. Mee
Directed by: Les Waters

The Gift Horse
By: Lydia R. Diamond
Directed by: Chuck Smith

2002–03 SEASON

Albert Theatre

The Beard of Avon
By: Amy Freed
Directed by: David
Petrarca

A Christmas Carol
By: Charles Dickens
Adapted by: Tom Creamer
Directed by: Kate Buckley

The Rose Tattoo
By: Tennessee Williams
Directed by: Kate
Whoriskey

Dinner with Friends
By: Donald Margulies
Directed by: Steve Scott

Gem of the Ocean
By: August Wilson
Directed by: Marion
McClinton

Bounce
Music and Lyrics by:
Stephen Sondheim
Book by: John Weidman
Directed by: Harold Prince

Owen Theatre

The Guys
By: Anne Nelson
Directed by: Robert Falls

Lobby Hero
By: Kenneth Lonergan
Directed by: Robert Falls

*The Christmas That
Almost Wasn't*
By: Child's Play
Touring Theatre
Directed by: June
Podagrosi

*By the Music of
the Spheres*
By: Carson Grace Becker
& David Barr III
Directed by: Chuck Smith

Trojan Women
By: Seneca
Translated by: David Slavitt
Directed by: Mary
Zimmerman

Latino Theatre Festival:
Festival Director:
Henry Godinez

*El Automovil Gris
(The Gray Automobile)*
By: Enrique Rosas
(from the silent film)
Directed by: Claudio
Valdes Kuri
Produced by: Teatro de
Ciertos Habitantes

*Mira'm "Se Dicen
Tantas Cosas" (Look at
Me "So Many Things
are Said")*
By: Marta Carrasco
Directed by: Marta
Carrasco & Pep Bou
Produced by: Compañía
Marta Carrasco

*Tengo Algo Que
Contarte Mi Amor
(Psst...I Have
Something to Tell You
My Love)*
By: Ana Castillo
Directed by: Henry
Godinez

*La Casa de Bernarda
Alba (The House of
Bernarda Alba)*
By: Federico García
Lorca
Directed by:
Marcela Muñoz
Produced by: Aguijón
Theater Company

The Maria Chronicles
Created by the
company ensemble
Directed by: Coya Paz,
Tanya Saracho,
& the ensemble
Produced by:
Teatro Luna

*El Mesajero (The
Messenger)*
By: Mayra Montero
Adapted by:
Cecilie D. Keenan
Directed by:
Edward T. Torres
Produced by: Teatro
Vista in association with
Okokan

2003–04 SEASON

Albert Theatre

*The Goat or, Who Is
Sylvia?*
By: Edward Albee
Directed by: Robert Falls

A Christmas Carol
By: Charles Dickens
Adapted by: Tom Creamer
Directed by: Kate Buckley

The Light in the Piazza
Music and Lyrics:
Adam Guettel
Book by: Craig Lucas
Based on the novella by:
Elizabeth Spencer
Directed by: Bartlett Sher

Crowns
Written and Directed by:
Regina Taylor
Adapted from the book by
Michael Cunningham and
Craig Marberry

Heartbreak House
By: George Bernard Shaw
Directed by: Kate
Whoriskey

Electricidad
By: Luis Alfaro
Directed by: Henry
Godinez

Owen Theatre

The Play about the Baby
By: Edward Albee
Directed by: Pam
MacKinnon

The Edward Albee
One-act Play Festival

The Zoo Story
Directed by: Lynn Ann
Bernatowicz

*The Death of Bessie
Smith*
Directed by: Chuck
Smith

*The Box, The Sandbox,
Finding the Sun*
Directed by: Eric Rosen

Marriage Play
Directed by: Louis
Contey

Proof
By: David Auburn
Directed by: Chuck Smith

Moonlight and Magnolias
By: Ron Hutchinson
Directed by: Steve
Robman

Latino Theatre Festival:
Festival Director: Henry
Godinez

*Culture Clash
in AmeriCCa*
By: Richard Montoya,
Ric Salinas &
Herbert Siguenza
Directed by: Tony
Taccone
Produced by:
Culture Clash

Let the Eagle Fly
Book by: John Reeger
Music and Lyrics:
Julie Shannon
Directed by: Ricardo
Gutierrez

*No Holds Barrio: an
intersection of Poetry
and Performance*
Written and Performed
by: Luis Alfaro

*Bodas de Sangre
(Blood Wedding)*
By: Federico
García Lorca
Directed by:
Marcela Muñoz
Produced by: Aguijón
Theater Company

Yuri Sam
By: Fábrica de
Teatro Imaginario
Directed by:
Ander Lipus

2004–05 SEASON

Albert Theatre

Finishing the Picture
By: Arthur Miller
Directed by: Robert Falls

A Christmas Carol
By: Charles Dickens
Adapted by: Tom Creamer
Directed by: Kate Buckley

I Am My Own Wife
By: Doug Wright
Directed by: Moisés
Kaufman

The Story
By: Tracey Scott Wilson
Directed by: Chuck Smith

Silk
Adapted and Directed by:
Mary Zimmerman
Based on a novel by
Alessandro Baricco

Dollhouse
By: Rebecca Gilman
Adapted from the play
by Henrik Ibsen
Directed by: Robert Falls

Owen Theatre

Hughie
By: Eugene O'Neill
Directed by: Robert Falls

Mariela in the Desert
By: Karen Zacarías
Directed by: Henry
Godinez

Ferdinand the Bull
By: Munro Leaf &
Robert Lawson
Adaptation and Lyrics by:
Karen Zacarías
Directed by: Marcela
Muñoz

*Floyd and Clea Under the
Western Sky*
Book and Lyrics by:
David Cale
Music by: Jonathan
Kreisberg and David Cale
Directed by: Michael
Wilson

2005–06 SEASON

Albert Theatre

Purlie
Music by: Gary Geld
Lyrics by: Peter Udell
Book by: Ossie Davis,
Philip Rose & Peter Udell
Directed by: Sheldon Epps

A Christmas Carol
By: Charles Dickens
Adapted by: Tom Creamer
Directed by: Kate Buckley

Pericles
By: William Shakespeare
Directed by: Mary
Zimmerman

A Life in the Theatre
By: David Mamet
Directed by: Robert Falls

The Clean House
By: Sarah Ruhl
Directed by: Jessica
Thebus

*The Dreams of
Sarah Breedlove*
Written and Directed by:
Regina Taylor

Latino Theatre Festival:
Festival Director: Henry
Godinez

Yerma
Produced by Aguijón
Theatre Company
By: Frederico
García Lorca
Directed by:
Marcela Muñoz

1001 Nights
Produced by:
Comedians

Blue Sweat
Produced by: Universes

Bichos do Brasil
Produced by: Pia Fraus

Ga-Gà
Produced by: Compañía
Marta Carrasco

Aiguardent
Produced by: Compañía
Marta Carrasco

Owen Theatre

Beyond Glory
By: Larry Smith
Adapted and Performed
by: Stephen Lang
Directed by: Stephen Lang

Romance
By: David Mamet
Directed by: Pam
MacKinnon

*The Revenge of the Space
Pandas or Binky Rudich
and the Two-Speed Clock*
By: David Mamet
Directed by: Steve Scott

The David Mamet Festival
One-Act Programs:

HOMECOMINGS
The Duck Variations
Directed by: Louis
Contey

*The Disappearance
of the Jews*
Directed by: Rick
Snyder

Home
Directed by: Louis
Contey

DAUGHTERS,
SISTERS, MOTHERS
Almost Done
Directed by: Ann Filmer

Reunion
Directed by: Ann Filmer

Jolly
Directed by: Rick
Snyder

Dark Pony
Directed by: Ann Filmer

GHOST STORIES
*No One Will
Be Immune*
Directed by: Steve Scott

The Shawl
Directed by: Mike
Nussbaum

*Crumbs from the
Table of Joy*
By: Lynn Nottage
Directed by: Chuck Smith

STAFF LIST

Robert Falls
Artistic Director

Roche Schulfer
Executive Director

Katherine Murphy
General Manager

Artistic Collective

Frank Galati
Associate Director

Mary Zimmerman
Manilow Resident Director

Chuck Smith
Resident Director

Regina Taylor
Artistic Associate

Henry Godinez
Resident Artistic Associate

Artistic

Steve Scott
Associate Producer

Tom Creamer
Dramaturg

Adam Belcuore
Casting Director

Tanya Palmer
Literary Manager

Administration

Peter Calibraro
Director of Finance

Deborah L. Clapp
Director of Management

Christopher Hipschen
*IT Director and Database
Administrator*

Richard Glass
Systems Administration

Deborah Grobe
Assistant to Ms. Murphy

Julie Massey
*Executive Assistant
to Mr. Falls*

Kristine Urnikis
*Executive Assistant to Mr.
Schulfer*

Jodi J. Brown
*Human Resources
Manager*

Kelly Ann Gray
Company Manager

Adam Goos
Ashley Jones
Business Office Associates

Development

Dorlisa Martin
Director of Development

Jeff M. Ciaramita
*Senior Director of
Administration &
Stewardship*

Kim Swinton
*Senior Director of
Major Gifts*

Janna Burch
*Director of Foundation &
Government Support*

Suzanne M. Griffith
*Director of Corporate
Support*

Jennifer Whittemore
*Director of Development
Services*

Leslie Garner
Premiere Society Manager

Melissa Hard
Annual Fund Manager

Victoria S. Rodriguez
Individual Giving Assistant

Bianca Delgado
*Corporate, Foundation &
Government Support
Assistant*

Shawn Rodriguez
Special Events Assistant

Kalena Dickerson
*Development Services
Assistant*

Sarah Harrington
*Assistant to the
Development Director*

**Education & Community
Programs**

Stacey Ballis
*Director of Education &
Community Programs*

Jessica Hutchinson
*Education and Community
Programs Assistant*

Marketing/Public Relations

Lori Kleinerman
*Director of Marketing and
Public Relations*

Jay Corsi
*Director of Advertising
and Sales*

Kimberly D. Furganson
*Marketing Associate &
Group Sales Manager*

Eleanor Berman
PR & Marketing Associate

Clare Asher
*Communications
Coordinator*

Nicole Gilman
Publications Associate

Lawrence Garcia
Michael Rashid
*Subscription Sales
Managers*

PUBLICITY
Denise Garrity
Publicity Director

Jennifer Dobby
*Associate Director of
Publicity*

GRAPHIC DESIGN
Kelly Rickert
Graphic Design Director

Tyler Engman
Graphic Designer

Facilities

Doug Jackson
*Assistant Facilities
Manager*

Richard Tenny
Custodial Supervisor

Miguel Melecio
Randy Sickels
Vernell Simmons
Custodians

Ticket Services

Robert Steel
Director of Ticket Services

Sabra Zahn
Ticket Services Manager

Erik Schnitger
*Assistant Director of Ticket
Services*

Summer Snow
*Assistant Ticket Services
Manager*

Eric Reda
*Special Ticketing
Supervisor*

Jennifer Shook
Ticket Services Supervisor

George Cederquist
*Group Sales
Representative*

Tim Gonzalez
*Ticket Services
Representative*

Operations

Mark J. Kozy
*Director of Operations
& Facilities*

Justine BonDurant
Front of House Manager

Chad Wachob
House Manager

Production

Scott Conn
Production Manager

Les Kniskern
*Associate Production
Manager*

Shera Street
*Assistant Production
Manager*

Stage Management

Joseph Drummond
Kimberly Osgood
Alden Vasquez
*Production Stage
Managers*

Sascha Connor
T. Paul Lynch
Stage Managers

Amanda Heuermann
Jamie Wolfe
Floor Managers

Scenic Art

Karl Kochvar
*Resident Scenic Artist,
USAA*

Scenery

Brian Phillips
Technical Director

Ryan Schultz
Chris Hopkins
Assistant Technical Directors

Rick Davalos
Scene Shop Foreman

Donald Bogart
Adam Derda
David Harkness
Jesse Moshure
Geoff Pender
Carpenters

Dwight Brooks
Sam Swartz
Assistant Carpenters

Steve Carlin
Scene Shop Assistant

James Norman
House Carpenter

Jess Hill
House Rigger/Carpenter

Properties

Alice Maguire
Properties Supervisor

Stephen Kolack
Properties Head

Christopher Kolz
Properties Carpenter

Nisara Thummamithra
Properties Artisan

Brendan Hendrick
Properties Assistant

Sabrina Pippin
Assistant to the Properties Supervisor

Electrics

Robert Christen, USAA
Resident Lighting Designer & Lighting Supervisor

Seth Reinick
Assistant Lighting Supervisor

Sherry Simpson
Electrics Head

Mike Durst
Patrick Hudson
Jay Rea
Electricians

Sound

David Naunton
House Audio Supervisor

Lilly West
Audio Head

Nick Keenan
Audio Technician

Costumes

Heidi Sue McMath
Costume Shop Manager

Laura Larsen
Assistant to Costume Shop Manager

Laura Mina
Assistant to the Costume Designer

Amy Frangquist
Hyunjung Kim
Stitchers

Birgit Rattenborg Wise
Head Draper

Dawn Joyce
First Hand

Susan Lemerand
Crafts

Jenee' Garretson
Wardrobe Supervisor

PHOTOGRAPHY CREDITS

The Goodman would like to acknowledge the following institutions and photographers for the images in this book:

Photo of past and current Goodman Theatre Board Chairs courtesy of Goodman Theatre, 20

Photo of rigging courtesy of the Goodman Theatre, 22–23

Photo of Edith-Marie Appleton courtesy of Albert Goodman, 18

Photo of Kenneth Sawyer Goodman and his daughter compliments of the Goodman Theatre archives, Chicago Public Library, The Harold Washington Library Center, 24

Photo of *Curse of the Starving Class* compliments of the Goodman Theatre, 27

Photo of *King Lear* compliments of the Goodman Theatre archives, Chicago Public Library, The Harold Washington Library Center, 27

Photo of Kenneth Sawyer Goodman's plays compliments of the Goodman Theatre archives, Chicago Public Library, The Harold Washington Library Center, 27

Photo of John Reich compliments of the Goodman Theatre archives, Chicago Public Library, The Harold Washington Library Center, 30

Photo of William Woodman compliments of the Goodman Theatre archives, Chicago Public Library, The Harold Washington Library Center, 30

Photo of the original Goodman Theatre compliments of the Goodman Theatre archives, Chicago Public Library, The Harold Washington Library Center, 30

Photo of Gregory Mosher and David Mamet courtesy of the Goodman Theatre, 33

Photo of Student Subscription Series courtesy of the Goodman Theatre, 138

Photos of the new building construction courtesy of the Goodman Theatre, 145

A Christmas Carol, 1978, courtesy of the Goodman Theatre, 142

The Goodman would like to acknowledge the following photographers for the images in this book:

Kevin Berne
Culture Clash in AmeriCCa, 93

Michael Brosilow
A Christmas Carol 2005, 142
A Life in the Theatre, 49, 85, 135
A Life in the Theatre Rehearsal, 40, 41
Dollhouse, 45
Electricidad, 91, 92, 126
Gem of the Ocean, 103
The Goat or, Who is Sylvia?, 125, 128
Hughie, 59
Pericles Rehearsal, 151
Proof, 85, 128
Proof Rehearsal, 150
The Story, 127

Lisa Ebright
The Amen Corner, 84, 85
Black Snow, 97
Fences, 100
The Good Person of Setzuan, 75
Millennium Mambo Rehearsal, 151
The Speed of Darkness, 49
The Tempest, 47
The Visit Rehearsal, 150

T. Charles Ericson
Jitney, 102

Eric Y. Exit
A Raisin in the Sun, 85
A Touch of the Poet, 59

Death of a Salesman, 61, 64, 65
Hollywood Arms, 119
The House of Martin Guerre, 114
Joe Turner's Come and Gone, 100
Journey to the West, 79
King Hedley II, 104, 105
Long Day's Journey into Night, 57
Ma Rainey's Black Bottom, 83, 128, 129
Pal Joey, 54, 55
The Piano Lesson, 103
Romeo and Juliet, 95
Seven Guitars, 101
Three Sisters, 132, 133
Two Trains Running, 99

Kevin Horan
Galileo, 36
She Always Said, Pablo, 74

Ken Howard
The Beard of Avon, 119
Sunday in the Park with George, 96, 134

Liz Lauren
Beyond Glory, 123
Black Star Line, 115
Blue Surge, 52
Book of the Night, 53
Bounce, 115
Boy Gets Girl, 97, 127
The Clean House, 127
Cry, the Beloved Country, 125
Drowning Crow, 89
Finishing the Picture, 63
Floyd and Clea Under the Western Sky, 125
Galileo Galilei, 77

The Gospel at Colonus, 117
The Iceman Cometh, 51
The Light in the Piazza, 113
Mariela in the Desert, 92
Mariela in the Desert Rehearsal, 150
Marvin's Room, 111
The Merchant of Venice, 119
The Night of the Iguana, 49
The Notebooks of Leonardo da Vinci, 12, 13, 78
The Odyssey, 80, 81, 127
On the Open Road, 50
Oo-Bla-Dee, 87, 88, 129
Pericles, 78
Play On!, 66, 67
Riverview: A Melodrama with Music, 53
Romance, 129
The Rose Tattoo, 120, 121
Seeking the Genesis, 115
Silk, 78, 131
Spinning into Butter, 109
'Tis Pity She's a Whore, 119
The Visit, 73, 75
Wings, 97
The Young Man from Atlanta, 51
Zoot Suit, 93

Steve Leonard
The Misanthrope, 47

Scott Suchman
Crowns, 88

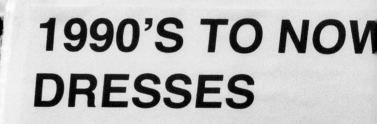

DRAG

1970'S
PRE
PAN
ENS

1970'S TO
PRESE
SE
1970'S
PRESE
VEST

DRESSES
full

bolo

unstru

blaze

eve
ja

2000's
Kristina/ as coat

evening wear
1980's

evenir
197

dresses
tailored &
career

DRESSES

KEY C
CLEANE

1970'S TO
PRESENT
EVENING WEAR

1970'S T
PRESEN
EVENING

1990'S TO NOW
DRESSES